Why a Duck?
visual and verbal gems from the Marx Brothers movies

Edited by Richard J. Anobile

Introduction by Groucho Marx
Preface by Richard F. Shepard

darien house, inc.
NEW YORK CITY

DISTRIBUTED BY NEW YORK GRAPHIC SOCIETY LTD., GREENWICH, CONNECTICUT

Pictures and dialogue from the following films are
used with the permission of Universal City Studios, Inc.
The Cocoanuts
Monkey Business
Horse Feathers
Duck Soup

All photos and dialogue from the following films
are copyrighted by and used with permission of
Metro-Goldwyn-Mayer, Inc.
Night at the Opera © MGM, Inc. (1935)
Day at the Races © MGM, Inc. (1937)
Big Store © MGM, Inc. (1941)
At the Circus © MGM, Inc. (1939)
Go West © MGM, Inc. (1940)

Standard Book Number 8212-0373-8

Library of Congress Catalogue Card Number: 73-159506

© Copyright 1971 Darien House, Inc.
37 Riverside Drive, New York City 10023

Designed by Harry Chester & Alexander Soma
Typography by Maurice R. Sinder

Printed in the United States

Introduction by
GROUCHO MARX

It was a few minutes before four in the morning, and I was tossing about in bed, regretting that, at the moment, there was no one around to toss. At the same time I was trying to make a decision: Should I drink a glass of warm milk and try again to sleep, or should I write an introduction to that book about the Marx Brothers—a book to be called —unless someone's kidding—**"Why a Duck?"**

Anyway, I was becoming wide awake; and since there's no money in drinking warm milk, I turned on the lights, sharpened a few pencils and started to write.

But Fate had other plans. At precisely four o'clock, as I was about to explain that the question, "Why a Duck?" came from a scene in " Cocoanuts", a scene between Chico and myself, I heard what sounded like a bomb exploding in the kitchen. And I, completely bewildered, did what any sensible American would do. I hid under the blankets. And there I remained until Hilda, my cook, called me. She said the hot water boiler had just blown up.

It was God's truth.

Hurrying into the kitchen, I found Hilda sitting on the refrigerator while the swirling flood waters splashed against her feet.

(Be frank, dear reader. Did you expect to see such fine writing in a book called **"Why a Duck?"** Can you imagine what this prose would look like if, say, Maxwell Perkins were my editor—just as he was for Scott Fitzgerald, Tom Wolfe or Sam Hemingway?

As for this Richard J. Anobile and his butchers who are editing **"Why a Duck?"** they actually had the nerve to tell me I'm getting "a trifle wordy."

The insulting bastards! Of course I'm getting wordy! Have they forgotten that I'm getting paid by the word? Just because I happen to be a sensitive dreamer who knows nothing about money, and cares less, they're trying to tell me that "Ha ha ha ha ha" is one word!

I'd like to remind this Mr. Anobile that if there are any words he doesn't consider worthy of **"Why a Duck?"** they will be snapped up by the Hot Rod Monthly.

Getting back to Hilda the cook—and about time —she remained perched on the refrigerator while I tried teaching her how to swim. She was not an apt pupil. But let's be fair. Not being able to swim myself, I was not an apt teacher.

As we waited—heaven help me—for the plumber, I thought a little enviously of the rich burghers on our block. With them it isn't the hot water boilers that blow up. It's their marriages. Here a man without three divorces is considered a nonentity, a failure. Why? Because it's obvious that he can't afford the luxury of maintaining two or more homes.

GROUCHO   CHICO   HARPO   ZEPPO

That's why the poor devil must stick to his first wife and his old boiler.

Don't get me wrong. I'm not suggesting that a first wife can't be fun. As a matter of fact I have some very wealthy friends who, if given their choice between a boiler blowing up and a marriage, would unhesitantly select the boiler.

It gives you something to think about.

* * *

You probably noticed that in a previous paragraph, I said "bastards" instead of "What the heck!" or "In a pig's eye!"

It's my way of trying to keep up with this changing world. To tell you the truth, I haven't done too well at it. When the Sexual Revolution began, I tried to enlist. But all I got was a series of humiliating rejections.

That was from the men. From the women came nothing but hysterical laughter.

At one time I did have a reputation for lechery (the leers and all). But I must confess it was all based on a misunderstanding. That and the fact that a cab driver in Chicago had a cold in his head and wasn't hearing too well.

I asked him to take me to the nearest book shop. He thought I said "hook shop."

***

I have been asked how I feel about nudity in the theatre. In the theatre—or any place—I love to feel about nudity. However, I'm greatly partial to female, American nudity.

In the past, if we wanted to see a few high-quality nudes on our stage or screen, we had to import them. This was, of course, economically unsound. I mean, why should a rich country like ours have to depend on one little French girl (Miss Bardot) for female skin when we have acres and acres of our own?

While we were saving the world for democracy (by losing three or four wars), a young GI stopped me in Dallas and said he didn't see how the Marxes could be brothers.

"For one thing," he said, "you fellows don't look alike. One talks with an Italian accent; one doesn't talk at all and the third talks too much."

(I didn't learn until many years later that this young man was Lyndon B. Johnson who, at the age of 26, was destined to become President of the Eureka Coal Company. But I wasn't surprised. There was something about the lad's eyes; the way he looked into yours; the firmness of his hand-shake and his warm smile that made you want to tell him the truth. What's more he showed us, without being asked, the deep scar left by his operation. You have to like a man like that).

***

I told Lyndon that I never learned how Chico became an Italian. God knows my father wasn't an Italian. But I will say this: he was probably the worst tailor in the history of New York.

As for Harpo, since he never talked, it was impossible to learn anything about his origin. I knew him only as the fellow who slept in the same room with Chico. We discovered that he was not dumb, except in money matters. He was just not crazy about conversation. Nor was he crazy about Chico, although they slept in the same bed, along with me and my mother.

***

I must not leave Harpo without some reference to his wonderful sense of sportsmanship. If, in chasing a blonde across the stage or screen, he caught her—and found her to be undersized—he would throw her back.

All this, I realize, does not explain Chico. Why did he talk with an Italian accent? Because, I believe, he thought Italian made him irresistible to women. And I think he was right.

Chico's Italian vocabulary was not large. Indeed I doubt that he knew more than a dozen Neapolitan phrases. But they were all useful. To give you a few examples, with their loose translations:

Bortcha motcha . . . ."Kiss me quick; I'm double parked."
Tutti Minooti . . . ."Help, help! I've been bitten by a snake!"
Dabisco si . . . ."Have you fed the cat?"
Ot'sa fine. . . . ."Ot'sa fine."

Unfortunately Chico's success with women proved his undoing. For one day backstage, when he was making considerable progress with a semi-Italian chorus girl, her husband, a drummer walked in and, being Italian Italian, beat Chico to a pulp. From then on Chico never again spoke Italian.

He spoke pure Pulp.

But I fear I'm digressing. Since this is meant to be an introduction to the Marxes and **"Why a Duck?"** (they really aren't kidding) I'll start with the brother I know best:

GROUCHO: He is modest to a fault. Shy, reticent, boyishly charming, he is handsome and—

Forgive me; that's the plumber at the door; and he gets paid from the moment he leaves his doorstep which, I believe, is in South Liechtenstein.

And the cook—good Lord!—she's still perched on the refrigerator.

Coming, Hilda!

Groucho Marx

Preface

by Richard F. Shepard
Cultural News Editor, *The New York Times.*

Ah, there were giants in those days. Along with Dodgers, Braves and Browns. But looking at antique flicks on the late show, or in little cinemas that specialize in films out of our past, reminiscing on S.J. Perelman reminiscing about Filmland Revisited, how can you ever doubt that there was a Special Breed then, something different from the faceless youths who today zoom into the lens on their motorcycles in monosyllabic search for identity?

Don't run away, youngster. This quavering octogenarian is not going to drivel on interminably about the Good Old Days, whose acronym is GOD. God is in his heaven and we are only reaching up to take out of the past what we can use today. To go way back is often fraught with peril. Well, it's certainly worth going back and fraught, if it lets us get onto the Marx Brothers. With all the current passion for dredging up the ancient in films, a pursuit of camp that ill suits this most campy of ages, it was inevitable that we would have to reckon with the Marxes, the sibling troika that dashed through the snows of twenty years lightly outrunning the wolves of weltschmerz that represented the Real World during the era of their dozen films.

They were actors, the most forgettable of creators compared to writers, composers, artists. If Mrs. Siddons or Sarah Bernhardt interest us today, it is because a biographer has made it so. We cannot really thrill to the memory of their performance because it is as extinct as a decalcomania after a rainstorm.

But film has done for the Marx Brothers (and others who went on camera) what no writer can do for the actor who faced only footlights. It has bestowed an immortality that is more part of us than part of them. We can still see them and it is like looking at "This Is Your life." The West Side movie house where I first saw "A Night at the Opera" is now a supermarket; yet seeing the film again not only gives me pleasure now but recalls the pleasure of seeing it then, on a dreary, rainy afternoon in a half-filled house that let me be the only one in my row, free to stretch out and laugh and laugh and laugh. It's all very sad to think about. I am starting to feel like Jean Gabin twirling a glass of pinard thoughtfully and about to utter something unspeakably and philosophically Gallic.

The job here is to make a Message out of all this. Remembrance of things past is alright for diaries and novels but Prologues have to plunge in and demonstrate that the topic at hand is important to civilization, humanity and the reader. It is the sort of thing most people do only for money, because it is a tough chore and usually inadequate to its design. Friends of the subject also do it for love, but even then they are solaced at least by minimum rates and promises of interviews on several dozen pre-dawn radio shows.

The most facile statement about the Marx Brothers and their movies would be to say that they were anti-Establishment. These days it is facile to say that almost anyone is anti-Establishment. Facile just won't do for the Marx Brothers. Their forte was to work within the Establishment, to be its court jesters, its cleansing and lusty Savonarola, destroyer of its

evils and protagonist of those who wanted the Establishment to work honestly and efficiently. They were dedicated to deflation, not disintegration. They were quick-relief-pill dispensers, not cancer surgeons. Complete antidisestablishmentarians.

There has lately been an inversion of roles between humor and society. Society is riddled with comedy, often lethal but funny nonetheless, and humor has become purposeful and serious, often deadly but unfunny nonetheless. The Marx Brothers could never be cast for a "Catch-22" or even a "MASH." Yet Groucho could certainly play a United States Senator straight, insisting that the mediocre American also deserves representation on the Supreme Court bench. In a world overstocked with leaders—civic leaders, community leaders, union leaders, ethnic leaders, cultural leaders, industry leaders and other loss leaders—we are immersed in unparsed grandiloquenxe worthy of Chico. Harpo is the sentimental ganef one hand patting you on the head and the other in your pocket—true to life but too trite to fit as modern humor.

So far, we've tossed a lot of technical terms around—Marx, Groucho, Harpo, Chico, film, life, humor and ganef, the usual panoply of jargon that clutters the quarterlies. It's only right that these should be defined for the reader who got into this bag under the illusion that he squander an evening in non-purposive laughter at some crazy movie characters. One can get committed for being so uncommitted, nicht wahr, Siegmund? Now that we've decided that the Marx boys are suitable grist for our modern mill, here's a word on who they are and what they did.

The three Marx Brothers were originally five plus a mother. None of them except Minnie, their mother, was known by the name they were born with—

at least not to their public. The first-born was Leonard. He was followed by Adolph, Milton, Julius and Herbert. On the job, they were known, in order, as Chico, Harpo (who had first changed his name to Arthur), Gummo, Groucho and Zeppo. The Marx pater was a tailor, but Minnie was Mrs. Show Biz. She had her children in greasepaint before they were weaned and organized herself and the kids, most of them still teen-agers, into a vaudeville unit. This shook down to the Four Marx Brothers. By the end of World War I (an insane bit of business for which they were not in the least responsible) they had been dubbed with their new names and Zeppo, who had been too young to start with them, had replaced Gummo, a man who apparently realized that there were more steady forms of income than those that came from letting simple folk laugh at you. But Zeppo was doomed to be the colorless Marx, and he, too, withdrew into the wings later.

They developed their style, incredibly, during a turn in Texas, when their audience walked out in midshow to watch a wayward mule outside. Disgustedly the brothers began to burlesque their own revue act and, mirabile dictu, the house bought it. In 1924, they left vaudeville and opened their own show, "I'll Say She Is," in New York. Alexander Woollcott, a critic more easily moved to tears than to laughter, saw them, loved them, touted them. The Marxes became an "in" property, but unlike current "in" hits, they wowed the outs, too.

In 1929, they filmed their stage success, "The Cocoanuts." It was a faithful adaptation, even to the extent of having painted backdrops easily spotted as such by the most oblique observer. But, of course, even the most oblique observer was watching the Marx Brothers cavort through the lobby of the Florida hotel where they were perpetuating their

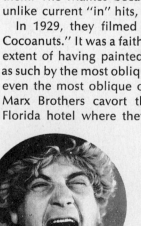

insults and japeries. A year later, they made "Animal Crackers," also from a stage comedy of theirs and the world came to know Captain Jeffrey T. Spaulding, the African explorer, who made a brilliant entrance in a sedan chair borne by natives and complaining that they must have come around the cape just to get a higher fare.

"Monkey Business," "Horsefeathers," and "Duck Soup" followed in short order and then in 1936 came "A Night at the Opera," with its classic scene of dozens of people crowding a stateroom small enough to have given Harry Houdini claustrophobia. Later, there were Marxist films such as "A Day at the Races," "Room Service," "A Day at the Circus" and "The Big Store," which was made in 1941. Then nothing until "A Night in Casablanca," in 1949, and "Love Happy," the film that ended the Marx team in the film business in 1950. It wasn't so much that the world had had enough of the Marxes, it was that the Marxes had had enough of Hollywood.

Whatever the three brothers were called in their movies, they played themselves and that was fine. They weren't always brilliant; they were only frequently hilarious in some of their movies. Groucho always sported the greasepaint mustache and, in his swallowtail coat, scuttled like a lascivious beetle (or how I imagine a beetle would scuttle if he were lascivious; it's hard to tell lascivious from non-lascivious beetles) emanating a con man's fraudulent aura of authority and put-down. Chico was too sympathetic a character to be a complete Italian joke, the kind that gets you picketed nowadays, but he was the literalist of word. Harpo, who never said a word, was the literalist of deed, a clown who, with pristine amicability, invariably ended up hanging his leg over the arm of the man of pretension. When Groucho said that Chico was the best argu-

ment for stricter immigration laws, it was a purely personal remark, not to be taken as a generic slur. Yet, when Groucho praised an Indian, "Red man, you're a white man," it was hard to tell whether he was making fun of the Indian or of the inane white cliche. There was no doubt what he meant, however, when the camera closed in on his wagging eyebrows and he looked at the audience and said, "The next number will be 'Come Where My Love Lies A-Dreaming'—with an all-male chorus."

As is well known (that's how the Pravda critic puts it), movies are rarely the work of the actors. The director fashions a film today. In the Marx Brothers day, the writers were the main ingredients. S. J. Perelman, George S. Kaufman and Morrie Ryskind were among the writers of Marx films. In other circumstances and perhaps in other books, these writers deserve the main play, but with the Marxes they were dealing with volatile elements who refused to follow scripts and insisted on inserting their own lines. Whatever it was, it worked. Very few other Hollywood actors could make that claim.

We are living through days when wit and wisdom (Spiro Agnew and Chairman Mao) must have applause cards, or else how would we know. It's hard to distinguish the stand-up comedian from the earnest and boring demagogue—the cigars look the same, whether it's the Catskills or Cuba. We are drowning in words. And what we really want is the security of something solid — perhaps Margaret Dumont, the frozen-faced grande dame who was the nearest thing to a Marx Brothers repertory player.

The Marx Brothers foreshadowed today's reality for us. They cannot be blamed that the reality is somewhat more joyless than their prescience. In their films, they appear as comic supermen, char-

acters of no past, no ties, no future. A vacuum is created and they rush in to fill it—a hospital head who is a horse doctor on the lam, a department store detective who revels in incompetence, an international statesman nuttily escalating tension. They return the status to a questionable quo by ousting the blowhards, the grasping, the baddies.

The Marxes were seminal performers. Even in the age of artificial insemination, it must be admitted that they were naturally seminal. Nobody like them appeared before they did. They initiated a style that has been imitated but never equaled. What, you ask, has all this got to do with you? What can the Marx Brothers do for you? They can make you laugh, dear reader, and if you're half the worried, beset, polluted, traffic-jammed, debt-ridden, family-bugged citizen that I suspect you are, laughter is not something that you can toss off lightly.

Notes on "Why A Duck?"

by Richard J. Anobile

I should have known better than to think small about the Marx Brothers. Two and one-half years ago this was to be a short, simple book of quotes and stills from their films, much like DRAT!, a book I had done on the humor of W. C. Fields. But, alas, the Marx Brothers done me in! I became so involved with their comedy that I began having guilt feelings about hatcheting my way through their films, plucking one line here and one line there and pawning it off as representative of their humor. So, faced by the bulk of what I had already accumulated, I decided to do what no one had tried—compile as complete a volume as possible by attempting a literal translation from celluloid to paper.

And so it came to pass. And so I came to realize why it had never been done this way before. My ego had long been telling me what an original and magnificent·idea this was and how I would revolutionize the presentation of film art in print. Pure bulldung. Bulldung? Putting two and two together and coming up with one big headache I soon realized that only pure and simple economics and practicality had prevented such a direct presentation. But by this time I was trapped; after all, I had already told my mother I could do it!

As you wander through this work you will note that there are hardly any production stills. Instead there are over 600 frame blow-ups. I wish I could be more precise as to the number, but if I had to count them one more time. . . . At any rate, the photos are all taken directly from the original films. All tolled I spent six weeks in Hollywood, both at Universal City Studios and Metro-Goldwyn-Mayer, running 35mm versions and marking each frame for the still departments. As I had selected nearly 1,200 frames there is no need to tell you that I endeared myself to the still departments. Each frame had to be cleaned, then made into a negative and finally blown to a print. The cost is still a thorn in my publisher's grouch bag.

Once in hand, the frames had to be put into sequence and finally matched with the actual dialogue as taken from the original soundtracks. The scene that proved to be impossibly difficult to bring together was the famed mirror sequence from "Duck Soup"; I had selected 58 frames to illustrate this scene. As there is no dialogue I could only reconstruct the action by running the film several hundred times. (That was the week eyewash stocks jumped to a new high.) Oh, by the way, don't you strain your eyesight looking for this scene here. I cut it from the book when I realized that it just wouldn't work on paper. Another blow to my ego, but what the hell!

I was hoping that this would be the most complete volume on this subject, but I had to settle for almost complete. From the earlier films, "Animal Crackers" and "Room Service" are missing. "Animal Crackers," now owned by Universal Pictures, is in a legal tangle. I tried my best to clear the rights for "Room Service" with the owner, RKO Pictures, but their corporate structure is in such a state that all attempts to clear rights were met by silence, evasion, or further excursions into the corporate labyrinth. I gave up. Fortitude is not my strongest virtue. As for "A Night in Casablanca" and "Love Happy," the last of the Marx films, I just felt, after several screenings, that the small amount of usable material would not warrant the time and money necessary to clear the rights. That is known as an editorial decision. I'll probably be hung by some picky Marx freak who will never forgive me these omissions—but that is the way of the world.

All the sequences in this book are complete in themselves. They were selected for their accommodation to the print medium. Some very funny scenes, such as the examining scene with Harpo, Chico and Groucho, from "Day at the Races," just could not make the transition. Rather than be complete I preferred the book to be fun.

The quality of the blowups from earlier films are inferior to those from the later MGM group. This is a technical problem that could not be overcome. As for "At the Circus," "Go West," and "The Big Store," you will note that there is very little used from them. Once again, editorial decisions. They yielded so little that if they too had been produced separately from the other MGM films I would not have bothered with them, but since I was already immersed in the MGM library, I used what little material I thought worked well.

Only one of my original assumptions was borne out through the work on this volume. No volume can ever replace the actual viewing of the films. How could it? However, sit back, flip through the pages, read the dialogue and couple this with your memories of their performances and I think you will find yourself laughing.

ACKNOWLEDGEMENTS

During the past couple of years I have met and worked with a great bunch of people. David Jacobson, President of MGM Merchandising, facilitated the fantastic cooperation I received from MGM; Ed Denning and his Universal City Studios legal staff, Joel Mann and Ernest Goodman, paved the way for me on their front. At MGM, Norman Kaphan and Bill Golden made still books and prints available to me. Don Kistler, a most patient and experienced film editor, suffered through my running and re-running of the films. Back at Universal, Sal Grasso helped greatly with stills, and Chuck Silvers, who rides herd over editorial, did a great job of making prints and fine-grains available and shuttling them to the Still Department where Grant Hough watched over the final product.

Making joint sense of all the photos and copy and assuring their presentation in a functional and graphically exciting manner was the difficult task of our designer, Harry Chester and his staff. As even a cursory glance through the pages of this book will reveal, they did a splendid job. In particular, it was Alex Soma who hurled himself into the task of creative design and whose knowledge of the films was a tremendous asset, which also made for a pleasant relationship between editor and designer.

I am also grateful for the help given me by Bob Hagel, Sharlene Collins, Robin Levine, Terri Yoshioka, Al Fusco, Barbara Yankevicz, and Stuart Solow. And last but not least, I thank Leonard, Adolph, and Julius, without whom there would be no book and a rather large void.

Richard J. Anobile

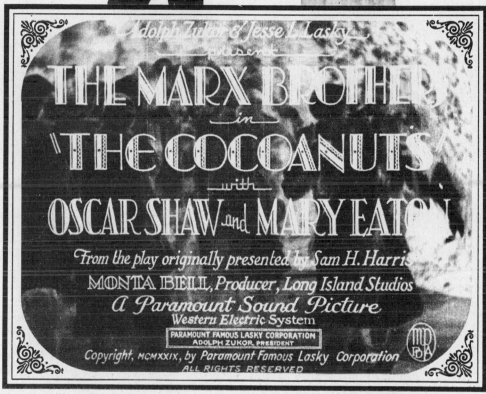

Mr. Hammer (Groucho) is approached by his staff at Cocoanut Manor and asked for a raise.

Bellboys: We want to see you, Mr. Hammer.
Hammer (Groucho): What's the matter? Somebody pay their bill?
Boys: We want our money.
Hammer: Yes — money — you want your money?

Boys: We want to get paid.

COCOANUTS

Hammer: Oh—you want MY money? Is that fair? Do I want your money? Suppose George Washington's soldiers had asked for money? Where would this country be today?

Boys: But they did ask.

Hammer: And where's Washington? No, my friends—no—money will never make you happy—and happy will never make you money. That might be a wise crack, but I doubt it.

Boys: We want our money!

Hammer: I'll make you all a promise. If you'll all stick with me and work hard, we'll forget about money. Let's get together and we'll make a regular hotel out of this place! I'll put writing paper in the hotel and next year if you behave yourselves, we'll have envelopes. I'm going to put extra blankets in all your rooms—free. There'll be no cover charge. Think—think of the opportunities here in Florida. Three years ago I came to Florida without a nickel in my pocket. And now I've got a nickel in my pocket.

Bellboy: That's all very well, Mr. Hammer, but we haven't been paid in two weeks and we want our wages.

Hammer: Wages? Do you want to be wage slaves? Answer me that!

Boys: No!

Hammer: Of course not. Well, what makes wage slaves? Wages. I want you to be free. Remember there's nothing like Liberty, except Collier's and the Saturday Evening Post. Be free, my friends. One for all and all for me—me for you and three for five and six for a quarter!

Mrs. Potter (Margaret Dumont) is accosted by **Mr. Hammer** who attempts to explain the positive side of Florida real estate.

Mrs. Potter (Margaret Dumont): How do you do, sir?

Hammer: Why don't you whistle at the crossing? You're just the woman I'm looking for. And now whether you like it or not, I'm going to tell you all about Florida real estate. It is the first time it has ever been mentioned here—today.

Mrs. Potter: I'm sorry, Mr. Hammer, but I'm afraid—

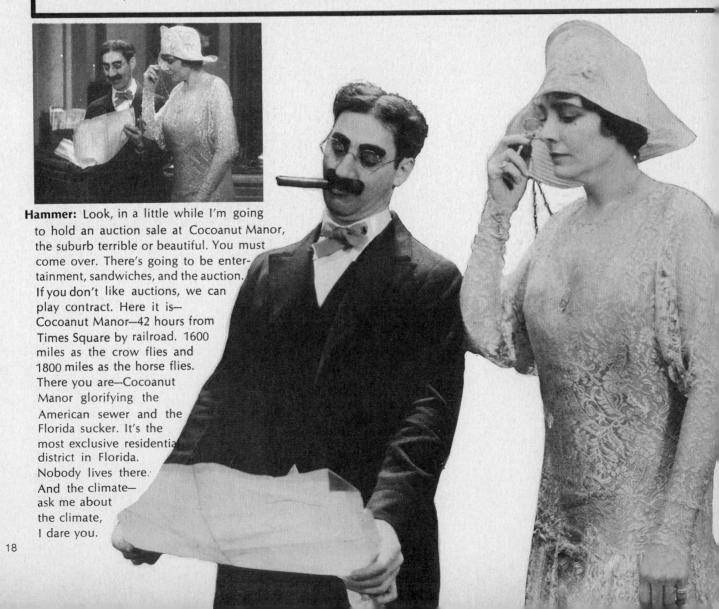

Hammer: Look, in a little while I'm going to hold an auction sale at Cocoanut Manor, the suburb terrible or beautiful. You must come over. There's going to be entertainment, sandwiches, and the auction. If you don't like auctions, we can play contract. Here it is— Cocoanut Manor—42 hours from Times Square by railroad. 1600 miles as the crow flies and 1800 miles as the horse flies. There you are—Cocoanut Manor glorifying the American sewer and the Florida sucker. It's the most exclusive residential district in Florida. Nobody lives there. And the climate— ask me about the climate, I dare you.

Hammer: Do you know that property values have increased 1929 since one thousand per cent? Do you know that this is the biggest development since Sophie Tucker? Do you know that Florida is

the show spot of America and Cocoanut Manor the black spot of Florida?
Mrs. Potter: You told me about that yesterday.
Hammer: I know but I left out a comma.

Mrs. Potter: Very well—how is the—
Hammer: I'm glad you brought it up. Our motto is Cocoanut Beach, no snow, no ice, and no business. Do you know that Florida is the greatest state in the Union?
Mrs. Potter: It is?
Hammer: Take its climate—no, we took that—take its fruits—take the alligator pears—take all the alligator pears and keep 'em—see if I care. Do you know how alligator pears are made?
Mrs. Potter: Haven't the slightest idea—
Hammer: There you are. That's because you've never been an alligator, and don't let it happen again. Do you know that it sometimes requires years to bring the pear and the alligator together? They don't like each other.
Mrs. Potter: No?
Hammer: No. Do you know how many alligator pears are sent out of this state every year and told not to come back?
Mrs. Potter: I don't think I do.
Hammer: All they can get a hold of. Florida feeds the nation but nobody feeds me and that's what I want to talk to you about.
Mrs. Potter: Mr. Hammer—
Hammer:—another thing, take our cattle raising. Oh, I don't mean anything personal. But here is the ideal cattle raising section. We have long horns, short horns and the shoe horns.
Mrs. Potter: Mr. Hammer, will you let me say something, please. . . .

Hammer: I hardly think so, and there's something else I want to bring to your mind. Where will you be when you're sixty-five? That's only about three months from now.
Mrs. Potter: If I were to buy, I should prefer some place like Palm Beach.
Hammer: Palm Beach? The Atlantic City of yesterday? The slums of tomorrow? Do you know that the population of Cocoanut Beach has doubled in the past week?
Mrs. Potter: Has it?
Hammer: Three bulldogs were born and we're expecting a nanny goat in the morning.
Mrs. Potter: I'm sorry, but I'm afraid I must be going.

COCOANUTS

Hammer: Aw, now, don't go. Before you go, let me show you a sample of the sewer pipe we're going to lay. Look at it. Nobody could fool you on a sewer pipe, can they, a woman like you?

Hammer: Now this is an eight inch pipe. But of course, all property owners will be allowed to vote on the size of their pipe. In case of a tie, it goes to the Supreme Court, and I can give you a little inside information in advance. The chief justice is crazy about this type of sewer.

Hammer: Here put it in your pocket— see you later.   **Mrs. Potter:** Mr. Hammer, I can't use this. I don't want it.

The doors swing open and in walk a pair of fig newtons—enter Chico and Harpo.

Chico: Hey. Come on. Come on.
Hammer: Gentlemen, how do you do? Come here.   Come here. What are you boys giving me, the run around? Come over here. Now, what do you want? What do you want? Explain your business.

COCOANUT*s*

Chico: We send you telegrams.

Hammer: Oh, you're the boys that sent these telegrams?

Chico: How do you do?

Hammer: That's a coincidence. I used to send telegrams myself.

Guest: How are you?

Chico: And how are you? That's all right. Don't worry.

COCOANUTS

24

Hammer: Say, you can stay, but you will have to take that ground hog out of here. Now what do you want? Explain your business.

Chico: Well, we want to make a reservash.

Hammer: Reservash?

Chico: Yes. We want a room, but no bath.

Hammer: Oh, I see. You're just here for the winter. Well step this way and I'll see what I can do for you.

Chico: All right. We stay for the summer, too.

Hammer: I'm sorry boys, but we got no vacancies.

Chico: Gota no vacancies?

Hammer: We got plenty of rooms.

Chico: Thatsa awright, we take a room.

Hammer: You want a room?

Chico: All right, we take a vacancy.

Hammer: Boy, take the gentlemen's baggage. Hey, hey, do you know that suitcase is empty?

Chico: That's all right. We'll fill it up before we leave.

Hammer: Oh, you will, eh? Well, you will empty it before I go out.

Hammer: Step right this way boys. Put on your moniker.

Hammer: This boy wins the gold cigar. Anybody else? Right this way. Hey, hey, hey, don't throw that. That's only for long distance.

Hammer: Now then what do you want? Would you like a suite on the third floor?

Chico: No. I'll take a Polock in the basement.

Hammer: You'll have to take that up with the Commissary Department, that's an entirely different proposition.

27

Chico: "He's hungry!"

A LOVE SCENE...

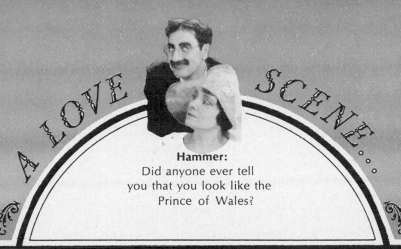

Hammer:
Did anyone ever tell
you that you look like the
Prince of Wales?

I don't mean the present Prince of Wales;
one of the old Wales, and believe me
when I say Wales, I mean Wales.
I know a whale when
I see one.

Hammer: Did you say your room is three eighteen? You know I am the proprietor of this hotel and I have a passkey for every room in it.

Hammer: Aw, if we could find a little bungalow—eh? Oh, of course, I know where we could find one, but maybe the people wouldn't get out. But if we could find a nice little empty bungalow just for me and you, where we could bill and cow, no — I meant we could bull and cow.

Mrs. Potter: Do you know what you are trying to say?

Hammer: Yes, it is not what I'm thinking of. What I meant was, if we had a nice little bungalow and you was on the inside and I

Mrs. Potter: Passkey?

Hammer: Passkey—that's Russian for pass—you know they passkey down the streetskey. Won't you lie down?

was on the outside trying to get in and me inside trying to get out or, no you're inside out and I was upside—I'll tell you, if you don't hear from me by next Friday, the whole thing's off!

Mrs. Potter: I don't think I understand.

Hammer: I mean—your eyes—your eyes, they shine like the pants of a blue serge suit.

Mrs. Potter: What? The very idea. That's an insult.

Hammer: That's not a reflection on you—it's on the pants.

COCOANUTS

COCOANUTS

Hammer: What I meant was if we had a nice bunga-low and I came home from work—and you standing by the gate—no—you'd come home from work—and I was standing by the gate, and we came down the path and we went inside and the shades were drawn and the lights were low, and then—are you sure your husband's dead?

Mrs. Potter: Why, yes.
Hammer: There seems to be a trace of uncertainty in that "yes." You know a yes like that was once responsible for me jumping out of a window and I'm not the jumper I used to be.

Hammer: What I meant was, you are going to be here all winter and I'm stuck with the hotel anyhow—why don't you grab me until you can make other arrangements?

Mrs. Potter: My dear Mr. Hammer, I shall never get married before my daughter.

Hammer: You did once! Oh, but I love you, I love you. Can't you see how I am pining for you.

Mrs. Potter: What in the world is the matter with you?

Hammer: Oh, I'm not myself tonight. I don't know who I am. One false move and I'm yours. I love you. I love you anyhow.

Mrs. Potter: I don't think you'd love me if I were poor.

Hammer: I might, but I'd keep my mouth shut.

Mrs. Potter: I'll not stay here any longer and be insulted this way!

Hammer: No — don't go away and leave me here alone. You stay here and I'll go away.

Mrs. Potter: I don't know what to say.

Hammer: Oh say, that you'll be truly mine, or truly yours, or yours truly. Don't you know what I'm—

Mrs. Potter: Will you keep your hands to yourself.

Hammer: Come on, I'll play you one more game. Come on the 3 of you.

Hammer: Oh, can you come down a little bit. Just think —tonight, tonight when the moon is sneaking around the clouds I'll be sneaking around you.

Hammer: I'll meet you tonight under the moon. Oh, I can see you now—
you and the moon. You wear a neck-tie so I'll know you.

COCOANUTS

COCOANUTS

**Chico is to be Hammer's shill at an auction—
if Hammer can teach him how to get to the auction.**

Hammer: Come over here, I want to see you. Now, listen to me. I'm not going to have that red-headed fellow running around the lobby. If you want to keep him up in the room, you'll have to keep him in a trap.

Chico: You can't catch him.

Hammer: Who is he?

Chico: He's my partner, but he no speak.

Hammer: Oh, that's your silent partner. Well, anyhow you wired me about some property. I've thought it over. Now, I can let you have three lots watering the front, or I can let you have three lots fronting the water. Now, these lots cost me nine thousand dollars and I'm going to let you have them for fifteen because I like you.

Chico: I no buy nothing. I gotta no money.

Hammer: You got no money?

Chico: I no gotta one cent.

Hammer: How're you going to pay for your room?

Chico: Thatsa your lookout.

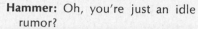

Hammer: Oh, you're just an idle rumor?

Chico: Well, you see, we comma here to maka money. I reada in de paper, and it say: "Big boom in Florida." So we come. We're coupla big booms, too!

Hammer: Well, I'll show you how you can make some REAL money. I'm going to hold an auction in a little while in Cocoanut Manor. You—you know what an auction is, eh?

Chico: I come from Italy on the Atlantic-Auction.

Hammer: Well, let's go ahead as if nothing happened. I say I'm holding an auction at Cocoanut Manor. And when the crowd gathers around, I want you to mingle with them. Don't pick their pockets, just mingle with them—and—.

Chico: I'll find time for both.

Hammer: Well, maybe we can cut out the auction. Here's what I mean. If somebody says a hundred dollars, you say two if somebody says two hundred dollars, you say three—

Chico: Speaka up?

Hammer: That's right. Now, if nobody says anything, then you start it off.

Chico: How'm I going to know when to no say nuthin'?

Hammer: Well, they'll probably notify you. You fool, if they don't say anything, you'll hear 'em, won't you?

Chico: Well, mebbe I no lissen.

Hammer: Well, don't tell 'em. Now then, if we're successful in disposing of these lots, I'll see that you get a nice commission.

Chico: How about some money?

Hammer: Well, you can have your choice.

Hammer: Now, in arranging these lots, of course, we use blue prints. You know what a blue print is, huh?

Chico: OYSTERS!

Hammer: How is it that you never got double pneumonia?

Chico: I go around by myself.

Hammer: Do you know what a lot is?

Chico: Yeah, too much.

Hammer: I don't mean a whole lot. Just a little lot with nothing on it.

Chico: Any time you gotta too much, you gotta whole lot. Look, I'll explain it to you. Some time you no gotta much; sometimes you gotta whole lot. You know that it's a lot. Somebody else maybe thinka it's too much; it's a whole lot, too. Now, a whole lot is too much; too much is a whole lot; same thing.

Hammer: Say, the next time I see you, remind me not to talk to you, will you?

Hammer: Come here, Rand Mc-Nally, and I'll explain this thing to you. Now look, this is a map and diagram of the whole Cocoanut section. This whole area is within a radius of approximately three-quarters of a mile. Radius? Is there a remote possibility that you know what a radius means?

Chico: It'sa WJZ.

Hammer: Well—I walked right into that one. It's going to be a cinch explaining the rest of this thing to you—I can see that.

Chico: I catcha on quick.

Hammer: That's a rodeo you're thinking of. Look, Einstein. Here's Cocoanut Manor. No matter what you say, this is Cocoanut Manor. Here's Co-coanut Manor. Here's Cocoanut Heights. That's a swamp—right over where the—where the road forks, that's Cocoanut Junction.

Chico: Where have you got Co-coanut Custard?

Hammer: Why, that's on one of the forks. You probably eat with your knife, so you wouldn't have to worry about that.

Hammer: Now, here's the main road, leading out of Cocoanut Manor. That's the road I wish you were on. Now over here—on this site we're going to build an Eye and Ear Hospital. This is going to be a sight for sore eyes. You understand? That's fine. Now, right here is the residential section.

Chico: People live there, eh?

Hammer: No, that's the stockyard. Now all along here—this is the river front—all along the river, all along the river—those are all levees.

Chico: Thatsa the Jewish neighborhood.

Hammer: Well, we'll pass over that.

Hammer: You're a peach, boy! Now, here is a little peninsula, and here is a viaduct leading over to the mainland.

Chico: Why a duck?

Hammer: I'm all right. How are you? I say here is a little peninsula, and here's a viaduct leading over to the mainland.

Chico: All right. Why a duck?

Hammer: I'm not playing Ask-Me-Another. I say, that's a viaduct.

Chico: All right. Why a duck? Why a— why a duck? Why-a-no-chicken?

Hammer: I don't know why-a-no-chicken. I'm a stranger here myself. All I know is that it's a viaduct. You try to cross over there a chicken, and you'll find out why a duck. It's deep water, that's viaduct.

Chico: That's-why-a-duck?

COCOANUTS

Hammer: Look . . . Suppose you were out horse-back riding and you came to that stream and wanted to ford over there, you couldn't make it. Too deep.

Chico: But what do you want with a Ford when you gotta horse?
Hammer: Well, I'm sorry the matter ever came up. All I know is that it's a viaduct.

COCOANUT∫

Chico: Now look . . . all righta . . . I catcha on to why-a-horse, why-a-chicken, why-a-this, why-a-that. I no catch on to why-a-duck.

Hammer: I was only fooling. I was only fooling. They're going to build a tunnel in the morning. Now, is that clear to you?

Chico: Yes. Everything—excepta why-a-duck.

Hammer: Well, that's fine. Now I can go ahead. Now, look, I'm going to take you down and show you our cemetery. I've got a waiting list of fifty people at that cemetery just dying to get in. But I like you—

Chico:—Ah—you're-a-my friend.

Hammer: I like you and I'm going—

Chico:—I know you like-a . . .

Hammer: To shove you in ahead of all of them. I'm going to see that you get a steady position.

Chico: That's good.

Hammer: And if I can arrange it, it will be horizontal.

Chico: Yeah, I see—

Hammer: Now remember, when the auction starts, if anybody says one hundred dollars—

Chico: I-a say-a two hundred—

Hammer: That's grand. Now, if somebody says two hundred—

Chico: I-a say three hundred!

Hammer: That's great!

Hammer: Yes. Now, you know how to get down there?

Chico: No, I no understand.

Hammer: Now, look. Listen. You go down there, down to that narrow path there, until you come to the—to that little jungle there. You see it? Where those thatched palms were?

Chico: Yes, I see.

Hammer: And then, there's a little clearing there, a little clearing with a wire fence around it. You see that wire fence there?

Chico: All right. Why-a-fence?

Hammer: Oh no, we're not going to go all through that again! You come along with me, and I'll fix you up!

COCOANUTS

Florida, folks—Sunshine—perpetual sunshine—all the year around. Let's get the auction started before we get a tornado. Right this way. Step forward. Step forward everybody. Friends, you are now in Cocoanut Manor, one of the finest cities in Florida. Of course, we still need a few finishing touches. But who doesn't? This is the heart of the residential district. Every lot is a stone's throw from the station. As soon as they throw enough stones, we're going to build a station. Eight hundred beautiful residences will be built right here. Why they are as good as up. Better. You can have any kind of a home you want to. You can even get stucco— Oh, how you can get stucco. Now is the time to buy while the new boom is on. Remember that old saying, a new boom sweeps clean? And don't forget the guarantee—my personal guarantee. If these lots don't double in value in a year, I don't know what you can do about it. Now we'll take lot #20—twentah—right at the corner of DeSota Avenue. Of course, you all know who DeSota was? He discovered a body of water. You've heard of the water they named after him. De Sota Water.

Hammer: Now this lot has a 20 foot frontage, a 14 foot backage and a mighty fine garage. Now then what am I offered for lot number 20. Anything at all. Anything at all, to start it.

Chico: Two hundred dollars.
Hammer: Ah—a gentleman bids two hundred dollars. Who'll bid three?
Chico: Three hundred dollars.

Hammer: Ha! Ha! Another gentleman says three hundred dollars. Do I hear four?

Chico: Four hundred dollars.

Hammer: Well, the auction is practically over. Yes, it's all over but the shooting. I'll attend to that later.
Chico: Five hundred dollars.

Hammer: Do I hear six hundred?
Chico: Six hundred-dollah.

COCOANUTƧ

COCOANUTS

Hammer: Sold for six hundred dollars. Wrap up that lot and put some poison ivy on it.

Hammer: Well, I came out even on that one. That was a great success. Yeah, one more success like that and I'll sell my body to a medical institute. Now, we'll take lot #21.

COCOANUTS

Hammer: There it is. There it is, over there, right where that cocoanut tree is. Now what am I offered for lot #21?

Chico: Two Hundred Dollars.
Hammer: Why, my friend, there's more than two hundred dollars worth of milk in those cocoanuts—and WHAT milk, milk from contented cow-co-nuts. Who will say 300?
Chico: Four hundred dollars. Five hundred dollars. Six hundred—seven hundred—eight hundred. What th' heck do I care?
Hammer: What the heck do you care? But how about me? Sold to what the heck for eight hundred dollars. I hope all your teeth have cavities and don't forget abscess makes the heart grow fonder.

Hammer: When he said via-duck, I should have smelt a rat. I did, but I didn't know who it was.

Hammer: Now we will take lot number twenty-two. What am I offered for lot #22?

50

Man: One hundred dollars.
Chico: Two hundred dollars.

Hammer: Sold for one hundred dollars!

Hammer: Believe me, you have to get up early if you want to get out of bed.

COCOANUTS

Paramount
PRESENTS

THE FOUR MARX BROTHERS
IN
MONKEY BUSINESS

Directed by NORMAN McLEOD

COPYRIGHT MCMXXXI by PARAMOUNT PUBLIX CORPORATION
ALL RIGHTS RESERVED

Groucho, one
of four stowaways,
tries his charm
on the captain
of the ship.

Captain: Hey, you!
Groucho: Are these your gloves?
I found 'em in your trunk. You
girls go to your rooms. I'll be
down shortly.

MONKEY BUSINESS

Captain: Who are you?
Groucho: Are you the floorwalker on this ship?
Captain: Floor—
Groucho: If you are . . .
Groucho: . . . I want to register a complaint.
Captain: Why, what's the matter?
Groucho: Matter enough. Do you know who sneaked into my stateroom at three o'clock this morning?
Captain: Who did that?
Groucho: Nobody, and that's my complaint. I'm young, I want gaiety, laughter, ha-cha-cha. I want to dance. I want to dance till the cows come home.

MONKEY BUSINESS

Captain: Just what do you mean by this?

Groucho: Another thing. I don't care for the way you're running this boat. Why don't you get in the back seat for a while and let your wife drive?

Captain: I want you to know I've been captain of this ship for twenty-two years.

Groucho: Twenty-two years, eh? If you were a man you'd go in business for yourself. I know a fella started only last year with just a canoe. Now he's got more women than you could shake a stick at, if that's your idea of a good time.

The captain is served a nervous breakdown as Groucho & Chico share his dinner.

Captain: Well, of all the colossal impudence!

Groucho: Why can't you stand up? Can't you see he has no chair?

Captain: Why—ugh—you—

Chico: You better keep quiet. We're a coupla big stockholders in this company.

Captain: Stockholders, huh? Well, you look like a couple of stowaways to me.

Groucho: Well, don't forget, my fine fellow, that the stockholder of yesteryear is the stowaway of today.

Captain: Well, you look exactly like 'em.

Groucho: Yeah? What do they look like?

Captain: One of them goes around with a black moustache.

Groucho: So do I. If I had my choice I'd go around with a little blonde.

Captain: I said, one goes around with a black moustache!

Groucho: Well, you couldn't expect a moustache to go around by itself. Don't you think a moustache ever gets lonely, Captain?

Chico: Hey, sure it gets-a lonely. Hey, when my grandfather's beard gets here I'd like it to meet your moustache.

Groucho: Well, I'll think it over. I'll talk it over with my moustache. Tell me, has your grandfather's beard got any money?

Chico: Money? Why, he fell hair to a fortune.

With the captain safely stashed in a closet, Groucho & Chico "invade the sanctity" of his quarters.

Groucho: How dare you invade the sanctity of the Captain's quarters?

Chico: I thought he was the Captain. Hey, I'm hungry. I'm a-lookin' for somet'ing to eat.

Groucho: I'll take care of that.

Groucho: Hello. Send up the Captain's lunch.

Chico: Hey, two.

Groucho: Send up his dinner, too. Who am I? I'm the Captain. You want to choose up sides?

MONKEY BUSINESS

Groucho: Oh, engineer, will you tell 'em to stop the boat from rocking? I'm gonna have lunch. Well, what's the matter with you?

Chico: What's the matter with me? I'm hungry. I didn't eat in three days.

Groucho: Three days? We've only been on the boat two days.

Chico: Well, I didn't eat yesterday, I didn't eat today, and I'm not goin' to eat tomorrow. That makes it three days.

Groucho: Well, state your business. I've got to shiver my timbers.

Chico: I got no business. I come up to see the Captain's bridge.

Groucho: The Captain's bridge? I'm sorry. He always keeps it in a glass of water while he's eating. Would you like to see where he sleeps?

Chico: Aw, I saw that. That'sa the bunk.

Groucho: You're just wastin' your breath, and that's no great loss, either. A fine sailor you are.

Chico: Hmm, you bet I'm a fine sailor. You know, my whole family was a-sailors? My father was a-partners with Columbus.
Groucho: Well, what do you think of that, eh? Your father and Columbus were partners?

Chico: You bet.

Groucho: Columbus has been dead four hundred years.

Chico: Well, they told me it was my father.

Groucho: Well, now, just hop up there, little Johnny, and I'll show you a few things that you don't know about history. Now, there's Columbus.

Chico: That's Columbus Circle.

Groucho: Would you mind getting up off that fly-paper and giving the flies a chance?

Chico: Aw, you're crazy. Flies can't read papers.

Groucho: Now, Columbus sailed from Spain to India looking for a short cut.

Chico: Oh, you mean strawberry short cut.

Groucho: I don't know. When I woke up, there was the nurse taking care of me.

Chico: What's the matter? Couldn't the nurse take care of herself?

Groucho: You bet she could, but I found her out too late. Well, enough of this. Let's get back to Columbus.

Chico: I'd rather get back to the nurse.

Groucho: Do you suppose I could buy back my introduction to you? Now, one night Columbus' sailors started a mutiny—

Chico: Naw, no mutinies at night. They're in the afternoon. You know, mutinies Wednesdays and Saturdays.

Groucho: There's my argument. Restrict immigration.

Groucho: So would I. But Columbus
was sailing along on his vessel—
Chico: On his what?
Groucho: Not on his what—on his vessel.
Don't you know what vessel is?
Chico: Sure. I can vessel. (Whistles)

Silence is Golden...

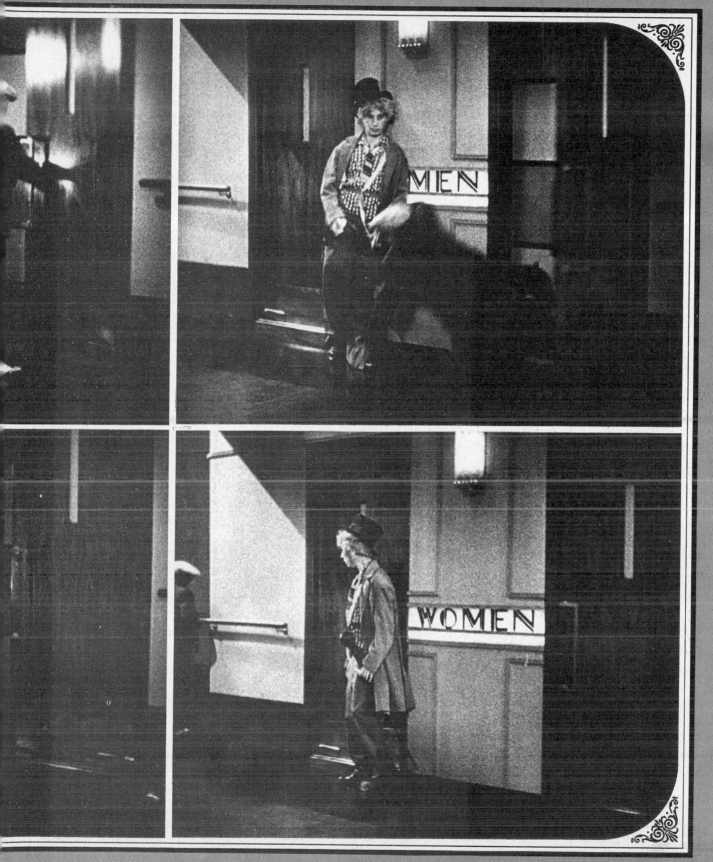

MONKEY BUSINESS

A couple
of cut-ups
decide to trim
a moustache—
snoop by
snoop.

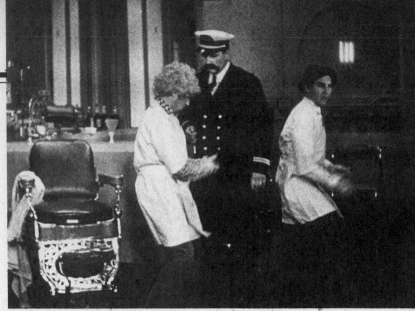

Chico: Well, how about a shave, huh?
Officer: Sure. Gimme a once-over.

Chico: Once-over, partner.
Harpo: (Whistles)

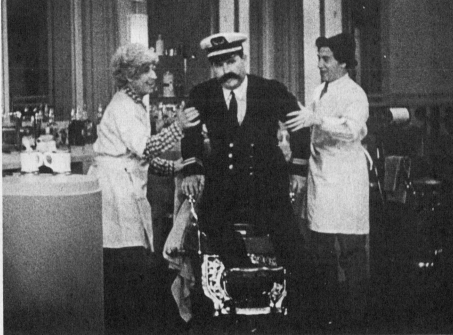

Officer: No, a shave.
Chico: On the face. All right.
Officer: Say, wake me up
   when you get through.
Chico: You bet. We take care
   of you, all right.

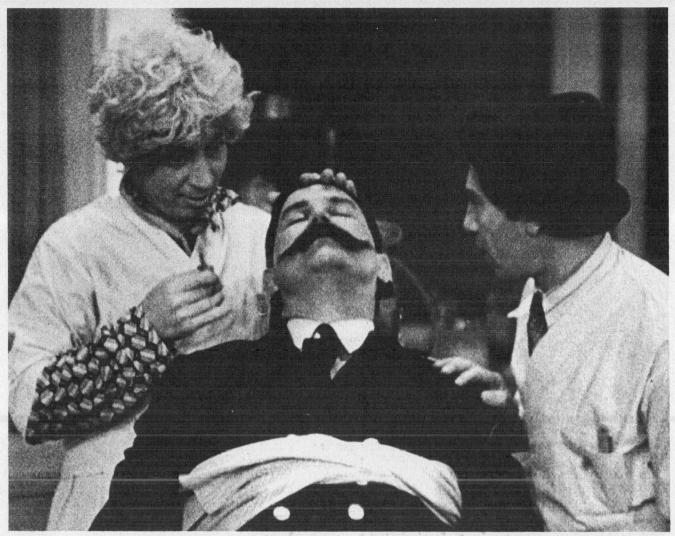

Chico: We take-a the tonsils last. I think we work the moustache first.

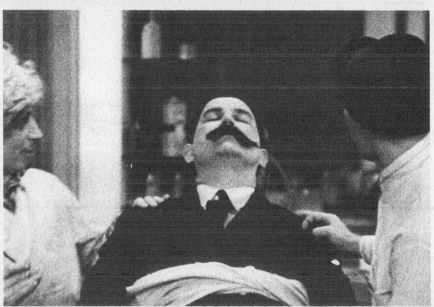

Chico: This side's too long.
Give 'im a little snoop.

MONKEY BUSINESS

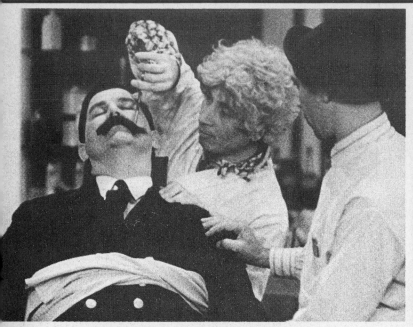 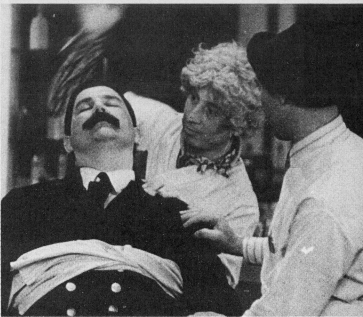

Chico: Give 'im a little snoop this side. Now, this side's too short. It's too short.

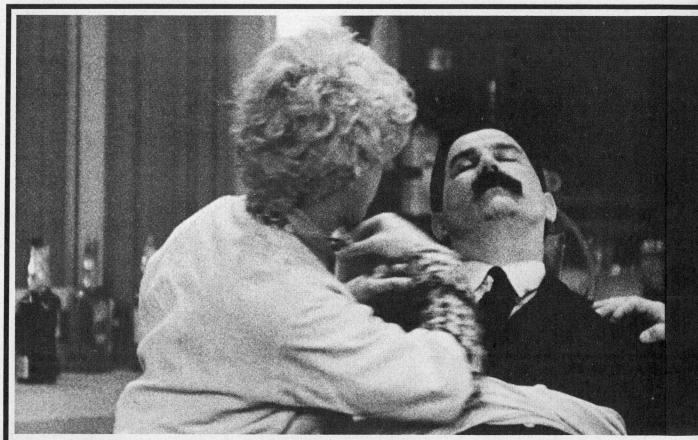

Chico: That's better, but the side's too short now is too long, the side's too long is too short.

MONKEY BUSINESS

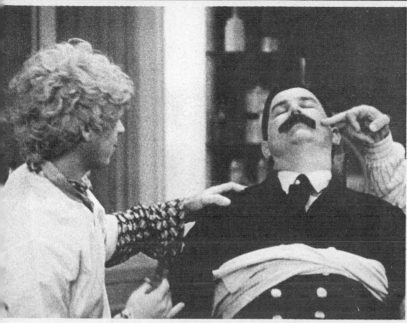

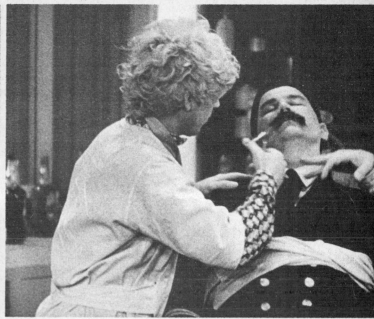

Chico: The other side is too long. Snoop 'im up.

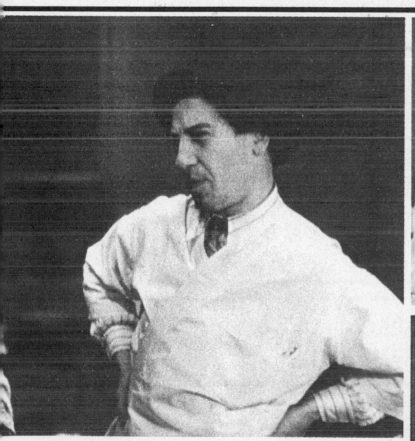

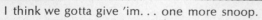
I think we gotta give 'im. . . one more snoop.

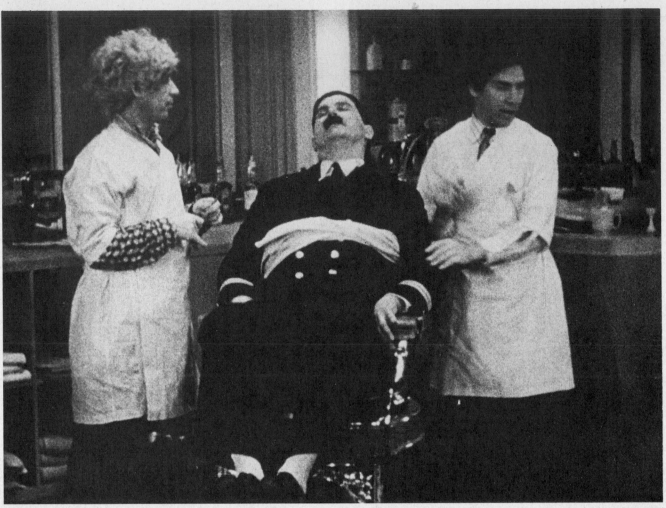

Chico: Think we better measure.

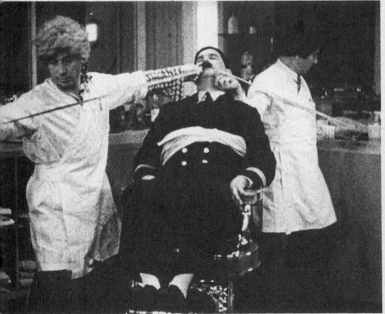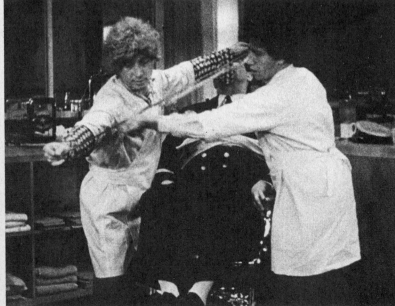

Chico: It's about a foot too much. Hey, no! The measure's about a foot too much! Now, looks much better.

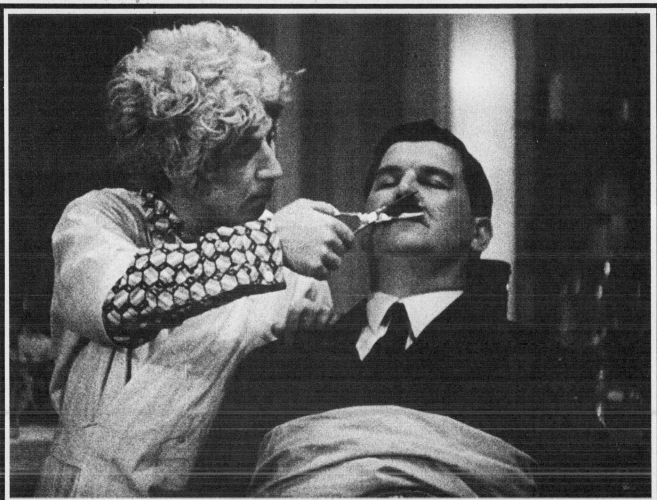

Chico: It can stand one more snoop in the middle, I think. In the middle, one snoop.

Chico: 'At'sa fine. 'At'sa very good.

MONKEY BUSINESS

Chico: I think—I think it's a little bit rough right here. I fix that.

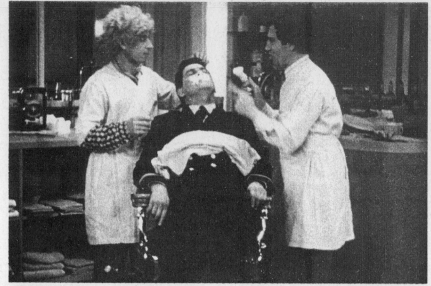

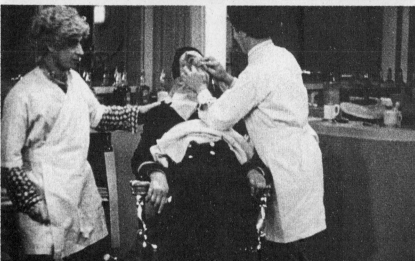

Chico: You know, I'm never goin' on this boat again. The food's no good. Of course, I don't eat yet, but even if I don't eat, I like the food good.
Harpo: (Whistles)
Chico: One more snoop. Hah! 'At'sa beautiful, hey? 'At'sa what you call a work of art. Hey, you know, I think you give 'im one snoop too much.

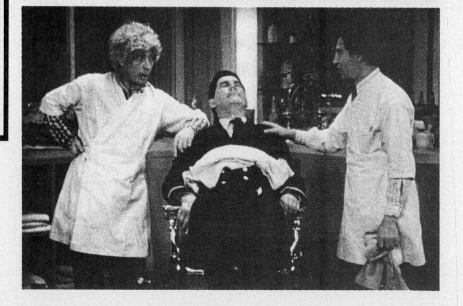

Groucho: Come on in.

MONKEY BUSINESS

Lucille (Thelma Todd) is going about her own business when Groucho pops out of her closet.

Lucille: You can't stay in that closet.
Groucho: Oh, I can't, can I? That's what they said to Thomas Edison, mighty inventor; Thomas Lindbergh, mighty flier, and Thomas Shefsky, mighty lak a rose. Just remember, my little cabbage, that if there weren't any closets, there wouldn't be any hooks, and if there weren't any hooks, there wouldn't be any fish, and that would suit me fine.

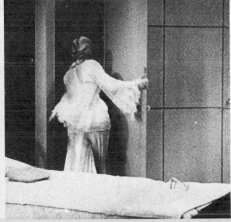

Lucille: Don't try to hide. I know you're in that closet.

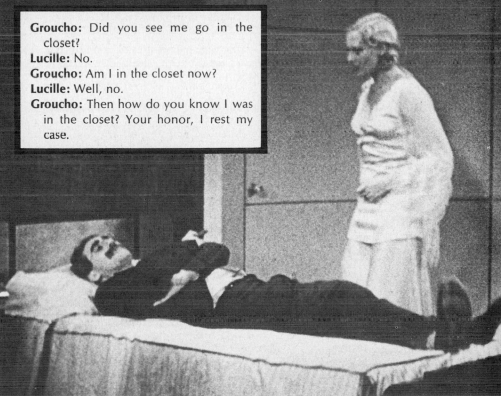

Groucho: Did you see me go in the closet?
Lucille: No.
Groucho: Am I in the closet now?
Lucille: Well, no.
Groucho: Then how do you know I was in the closet? Your honor, I rest my case.

MONKEY BUSINESS

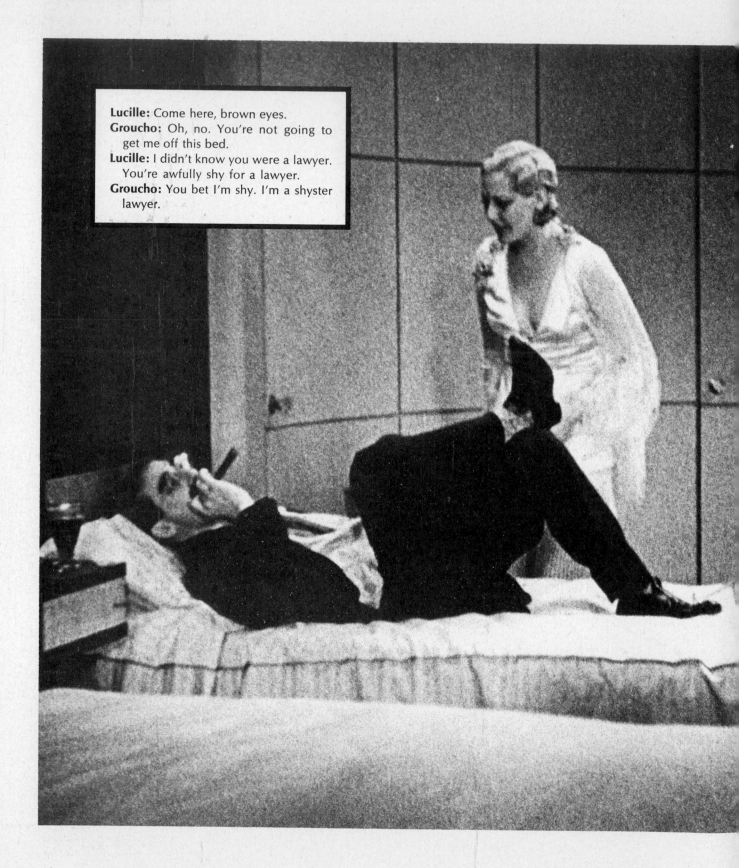

Lucille: Well, then, what do you think of an egg that would give me—

Groucho: I know—I know. You're a woman who's been getting nothing but dirty breaks. Well, we can clean and tighten your brakes, but you'll have to stay in the garage all night.

Lucille: I want excitement. I want to ha-cha-cha-cha. You don't realize it . . .

MONKEY BUSINESS

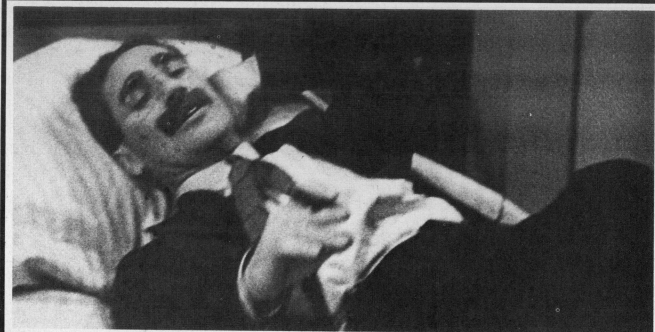

Lucille: . . . but from the time he got the marriage license, I've led a dog's life.

Groucho: Are you sure he didn't get a dog's license?

Lucille: Oh, Alky can't make a fool of me. I want to go places. I want to do things. I want freedom, I want liberty, I want justice—

Groucho: Ta-ra-ta-da-da- etc. Madam, you're making history. In fact, you're making me, and I wish you'd keep my hands to yourself.

Lucille: Oh, you know what I want. I want life, I want laughter, I want gaiety. I want to ha-cha-cha-cha.

Groucho: Madam, before I get through with you, you will have a clear case for divorce, and so will my wife. Now, the first thing to do is to arrange for a settlement. You take the children, your husband takes the house, Junior burns down the house, you take the insurance, and I take you.

Lucille: But I haven't any children.

Groucho: That's just the trouble with this country. You haven't any children, and as for me, I'm going back in the closet where men are empty overcoats.

Groucho: And you can say it was a real love match. We married for money.

Madame: Oh, you impudent cad!

Groucho: Eh, my shrinking violet? Say, it wouldn't hurt you to shrink thirty or forty pounds.

Madame: I'll report you to your paper.

Groucho: I'll thank you to let me do the reporting. Is it true you're getting a divorce as soon as your husband recovers his eyesight? Is it true you wash your hair in clam broth? Is it true you used to dance in a flea circus.?

Madame: This is outrageous! If you don't stop, I'll call the Captain.
Groucho: Oh, so that's it. Infatuated with a pretty uniform! We don't count, after we've given you the best years of our lives. You have to have an officer.

Madame: I don't like this innuendo.
Groucho: That's what I always say. Love flies out the door when money comes innuendo. Well, goodbye. It's nice to have seen you, but I've got nobody to blame but myself. Ta-ta.

Man: Doctor! Doctor! Are you a doctor?
Groucho: Sure, I'm a doctor. Where's the horse?

Man: Why, a man fainted over here.
Groucho: Man fainted. I'll soon fix him. Just my —hard luck it couldn't be a woman!

Groucho: Hmmm. Just as I thought—smoking too much.
Man: Here he is doctor!
Groucho: Don't tell me. I'll find him myself.

MONKEY BUSINESS

Groucho: I can't do anything for that man. He's fainted. What he needs is an ocean voyage.

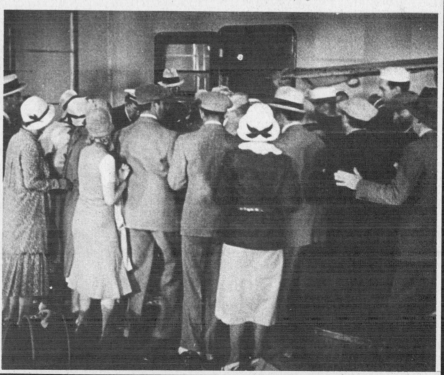

Groucho: In the meantime, get him off the boat and have his baggage examined.

Man: Gangway.

Groucho: Will you all get close so he won't recover? Here, right this way. Step right around here.

ANOTHER LOVE SCENE

Groucho:
How about you
and I passing out on the
veranda, or would you rather
pass out here?

Woman: Sir, you have the
advantage of me!
Groucho: Not yet I haven't,
but wait till I get you
outside.

MONKEY BUSINESS

Groucho proves there's nothing money can't buy.

Groucho: Hey!   **Butler:** Yes, sir?

Butler: Oh! Oh, no, sir. This is special for Mr. Helton, sir.

Groucho: You see this?

Groucho: Come back in a half hour and I'll give you another look at it.

MONKEY BUSINESS

Groucho
courts Lucille
on the
veranda.

M-E-E-E-O-W

87

Groucho: Me-e-e-ow

Groucho: Me-e-e-ow. Meow!

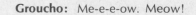

Groucho: Me-e-e-ow!
Lucille: What brought you here?
Groucho: Ah, 'tis midsummer madness, the music is in my temples, the hot blood of youth! Come, Kapellmeister, let the violas throb. My regiment leaves at dawn!

MONKEY BUSINESS

Groucho: Aw, I guess my regiment can go without me!

Lucille: Oh, no, no, no, don't. My husband might be inside, and if he finds me out here he'll wallop me.
Groucho: Always thinking of your husband.   Couldn't I wallop you just as well?

89

Lucille: Oh, I heard Alky talking about this party.

Groucho: Oh, I've dreamed of a night like this, I tell you. Now, you tell me about some of your dreams.

Lucille: Dreams! Ha! I can't even sleep anymore wondering who he's chasing around with.

Groucho: Oh, why can't we break away from all this, just you and I, and lodge with my fleas in the hills? I mean, flee to my lodge in the hills.

Lucille: Oh, no, I couldn't think of it.

Groucho: Don't be afraid. You can join this lodge for a few pennies, and you won't even have to take a physical examination, unless you insist on one.

Lucille: What a swell home life I've got. Why, I think I'd almost marry you to spite that double-crossing crook.

Groucho: Mrs. Briggs, I've known and respected your husband, Alky, for many years, and what's good enough for him is good enough for me.

Lucille: Ugh!

Man: Oh, Emily!
Woman: Oh, Henry, be careful. Somebody may see us.
Man: Oh, I've been careful too long.

Groucho: Well, now that you brought that up, just how long have you been careful?
Woman: Oh, they saw us!
Man: Now be calm, Emily. I'll talk to them. You won't say anything about this, will you?

MONKEY BUSINESS

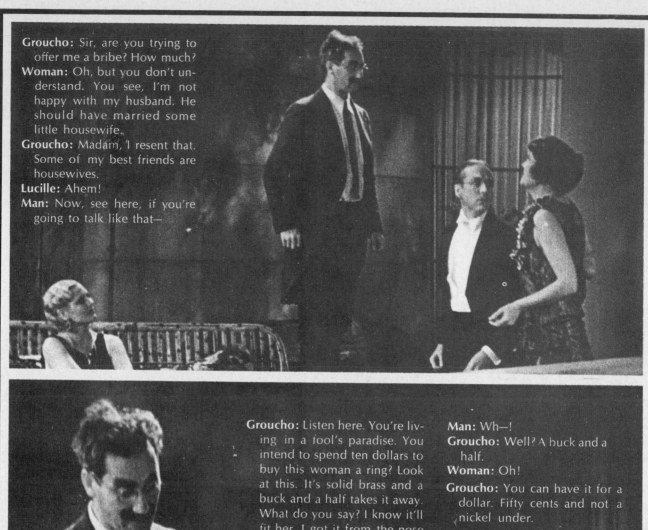

Groucho: Sir, are you trying to offer me a bribe? How much?

Woman: Oh, but you don't understand. You see, I'm not happy with my husband. He should have married some little housewife.

Groucho: Madam, I resent that. Some of my best friends are housewives.

Lucille: Ahem!

Man: Now, see here, if you're going to talk like that—

Groucho: Listen here. You're living in a fool's paradise. You intend to spend ten dollars to buy this woman a ring? Look at this. It's solid brass and a buck and a half takes it away. What do you say? I know it'll fit her. I got it from the nose of a savage.

Man: Wh—!

Groucho: Well? A buck and a half.

Woman: Oh!

Groucho: You can have it for a dollar. Fifty cents and not a nickel under.

MONKEY BUSINESS

Groucho: Now then, my friends, what am I offered for this fine piece of French bric-a-brac?

Lucille: Oh, I know what it is... to be unhappy.

Groucho: How do you think I feel? Here I am stuck with this ring.

Groucho: No, you're wrong, girls. You're wrong. In the first place, Gary Cooper is much taller than I am.

Groucho: I wish to announce that a buffet supper will be served in the next room in five minutes. In order to get you in that room quickly, Mrs. Schmalhausen will sing a soprano solo in this room.

MONKEY BUSINESS

DIRECTED BY

NORMAN McLEOD

COPYRIGHT MCMXXXII by PARAMOUNT PUBLIX CORPORATION
ALL RIGHTS RESERVED

Huxley College is to have a new president. The film opens as Professor Quincy Adams Wagstaff (Groucho) takes over.

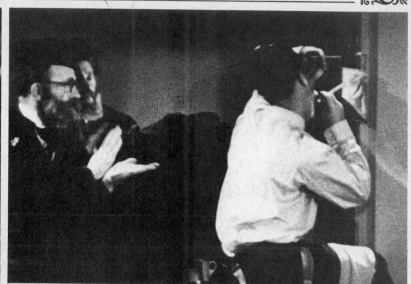

Professor: And so, in retiring as president of this college, it is indeed a painful task to bid you all goodbye. And now, with the utmost pleasure, may I present to you the man who is to guide the destinies of this great institution . . . Professor Quincy Adams Wagstaff.

Professor: Professor, it is indeed an honor to welcome you to Huxley College.   **Wagstaff:** Never mind that. Hold this coat.

Professor: By the way, Professor, there is no smoking.
Wagstaff: That's what **you** said.
Professor: It would please the faculty if you would throw your cigar away.

Wagstaff: The faculty members might just as well keep their seats. There'll be no diving for this cigar. Ahem!

HORSEFEATHERS

As I look out over your eager faces I can readily understand why this college is flat on its back. The last college I presided over things were slightly different. I was flat on my back. Things kept going from bad to worse, but we all put our shoulders to the wheel, and it wasn't long before I was flat on my back again. Any questions? Any answers? Any rags, any bones, any bottles today? Any rags—

Let's have some action around here. Who'll say seventy-six? Who'll say seventeen seventy-six? That's the spirit, seventeen seventy-six.

98

Wagstaff: No doubt you would like to know why I am here. I came into this college to get my son out of it.

Wagstaff: I remember the day he left to come here, a mere boy and a beardless youth. I kissed them both goodbye.

Wagstaff: By the way, where is my son?

HORSEFEATHERS

Wagstaff: Young lady, would you mind getting up so I can see the son rise?

Wagstaff: So, doing your home work in school, eh?

Frank (Zeppo): Hello, old timer.

HORSEFEATHERS

Professor: My dear Professor, I'm sure the students would appreciate a brief outline of your plans for the future.
Wagstaff: What?
Professor: I said the students would appreciate a brief outline of your plans for the future.
Wagstaff: You just said that. That's the trouble around here. Talk, talk, talk! Oh, sometimes I think I must go mad. Where will it all end? What is it getting you?

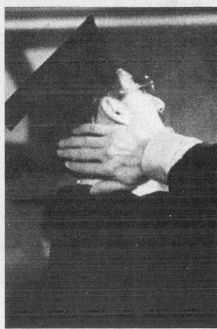

Wagstaff: Why don't you go home to your wife? I'll tell you what. I'll go home to your wife and outside of the improvements, she'll never know the difference. Pull over to the side of the road there and let me see your marriage license.

Professor: Professor Wagstaff, now that you have stepped into my shoes . . .

Wagstaff: Oh, is that what I stepped in? I wondered what it was. If these are your shoes, the least you can do is have 'em cleaned.

Professor: The trustees have a few suggestions they would like to submit to you.

Wagstaff: I think you know what the trustees can do with their suggestions.

HORSEFEATHERS

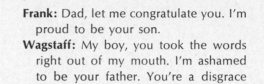

Frank: Dad, let me congratulate you. I'm proud to be your son.

Wagstaff: My boy, you took the words right out of my mouth. I'm ashamed to be your father. You're a disgrace to our family name of Wagstaff, if such a thing is possible.

Wagstaff: What's all this talk I hear about you fooling around with the college widow? No wonder you can't get out of college. Twelve years in one college! I went to three colleges in twelve years and fooled around with three college widows. When I was your age I went to bed right after supper. Sometimes I went to bed before supper. Sometimes I went without my supper and didn't go to bed at all.

Wagstaff: A college widow stood for something in those days. In fact, she stood for plenty!

Frank: There's nothing wrong between me and the college widow.

Wagstaff: There isn't, huh? Then you're crazy to fool around with her!

Frank: Aw, but you don't—

Wagstaff: I don't want to talk to you about this again, you snob. I'd horsewhip you if I had a horse. You may go now. Leave your name and address with the girl outside and if anything turns up we'll get in touch with you.

HORSEFEATHERS

Wagstaff: Where're you going?
Frank: Well, you just told me to go.

Wagstaff: So that's what they taught you in college! Just when I tell you to go, you leave me. You know you can't leave a school room without raising your hand, no matter where you're going.

Frank: Dad, this college has had a new president every year since 1888.
Wagstaff: Yeah.
Frank: And that's the year we won our last football game. Now, I like education as well as the next fellow—
Wagstaff: Well, move over and I'll talk to the next fellow.
Frank: But a college needs something else besides education. And what this college needs is a good football team, and you can't have a good football team unless you have good football players.
Wagstaff: My boy . . . I think you've got something there, and I'll wait outside until you clean it up. I know it's dangerous, but I'm going to ask you one more question. Where do you get good football players?
Frank: Well, in a speakeasy down . . .

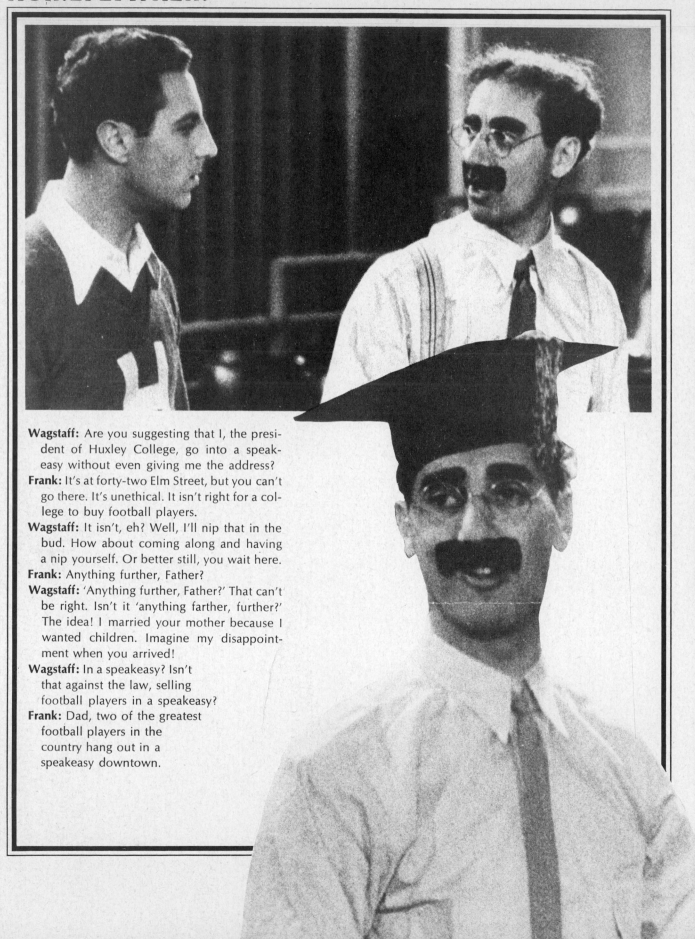

Wagstaff: Are you suggesting that I, the president of Huxley College, go into a speakeasy without even giving me the address?

Frank: It's at forty-two Elm Street, but you can't go there. It's unethical. It isn't right for a college to buy football players.

Wagstaff: It isn't, eh? Well, I'll nip that in the bud. How about coming along and having a nip yourself. Or better still, you wait here.

Frank: Anything further, Father?

Wagstaff: 'Anything further, Father?' That can't be right. Isn't it 'anything farther, further?' The idea! I married your mother because I wanted children. Imagine my disappointment when you arrived!

Wagstaff: In a speakeasy? Isn't that against the law, selling football players in a speakeasy?

Frank: Dad, two of the greatest football players in the country hang out in a speakeasy downtown.

The password is "Swordfish". Baravelli (Chico) has it; Wagstaff has to get it.

Baravelli: Who are you?
Wagstaff: I'm fine, thanks. Who are you?
Baravelli: I'm fine, too, but you can't come in unless you give the password.

Wagstaff: Well, what is the password?

Baravelli: Oh, no, you gotta tell me. Hey, I tell you what I do. I give you three guesses. It's the name of a fish.

Wagstaff: Is it Mary?

Baravelli: (Laughs) 'At's no fish.

Wagstaff: She isn't? Well, she drinks like one. Let me see, is it sturgeon?

Baravelli: Hey, you crazy? Sturgeon's a doctor cuts you open when you're sick.

Baravelli: Now, I give you one more chance.

Wagstaff: I got it! Haddock.

Baravelli: 'At's funny, I gotta haddock, too.

Wagstaff: What do you take for a haddock?

Baravelli: Well, sometimes I take-a aspirin, sometimes I take a calomel.

Wagstaff: Say, I'd walk a mile for a calomel.

Baravelli: You mean chocolate calomel? I like that, too, but you no guess it.

Baravelli: Hey, what'sa matter? You no understand English? You can't come in here unless you say swordfish. Now, I give you one more guess.

Wagstaff: Swordfish, swordfish. I think I got it. Is it swordfish?
Baravelli: Heh! That's it. You guess it.
Wagstaff: Pretty good, eh?
Baravelli: Fine, you guess it. All right.

Wagstaff: What do you want?
Baravelli: I wanna come in.
Wagstaff: What's the password?
Baravelli: Aw, you no fool me. Heh! Swordfish.

Wagstaff: No, I got tired of that. I changed it.
Baravelli: Well, what is the password now?
Wagstaff: Say, I forgot it. I'd better come outside with you.

Bum: Say, buddy, could you help me out? I'd like to get a cup of coffee.

HORSEFEATHERS

Wagstaff decides to draft some pros for his college team. The offer is tendered and the deal is closed.

Baravelli: Well, first we want a football.

Wagstaff: Well, I don't know if we've got a football, but if I can find one, would you be interested? I don't want a hasty answer, just sleep on it.

Baravelli: I no think I can sleep on a football.

Wagstaff: Well, let's get down to business. I'm looking for two football players who always hang around here.

Baravelli: We always hang around here, but we don't—

Wagstaff: Well, that's all I want to know. I'm Professor Wagstaff of Huxley College.

Baravelli: That means nothing to me.

Wagstaff: Well, it doesn't mean anything to me, either.

Wagstaff: I'll try it over again. I'm Professor Huxley of Wagstaff College.

Baravelli: Well, you didn't stay at the other college very long.

Wagstaff: You're heading for a breakdown. Why don't you pull yourself to pieces?

Wagstaff: In case I never see you again, which would add ten years to my life, what would you fellows want to play football?

Bartender: Who's gonna settle for these drinks?

Baravelli: You're stuck.

Wagstaff: Can you cash a check for fifteen dollars and twenty-two cents?

Bartender: Sure. Five, ten, fifteen and twenty-two.

Wagstaff: Thanks. As soon as I get a check for fifteen dollars and twenty-two cents, I'll send it to you. Swordfish!

HORSEFEATHERS

Wagstaff: That's a fine way to carry ice. Where are your tongs? Looks like a tong war!

117

HORSEFEATHERS

Baravelli: Well, that's the last time we deliver ice unless you pay the bill.
Wagstaff: How much do we owe you?
Baravelli: Two thousand dollars.
Wagstaff: Two thousand dollars for ice? I can get an Eskimo for two hundred dollars and make my own ice.

Meanwhile...

Baravelli: I tell you what we do. I make you a proposition. You owe us two hundred dollars. We take two thousand and call it square.

Wagstaff: That's not a bad idea. I tell you, I'll consult my lawyer and if he advises me to do it, I'll get a new lawyer. Why don't you forget about the money? Go to college, meet all the beautiful girls, get yourself a co-ed.

Baravelli: Hah! I got a co-ed. Last week for eighteen dollars I got a co-ed with two pair of pants.

Wagstaff: Since when has a co-ed got two pair of pants?

Baravelli: Since I joined the college.

Wagstaff: Baravelli, you've got the brain of a four-year-old boy, and I bet he was glad to get rid of it.

Wagstaff: Well, now that you're a college boy, here's your hat, here's your pennant, here's your coat. All right, report for football practice in the morning. Now, I want you to sign this agreement.

Baravelli: Hey, there's nothing on this paper.

Wagstaff: That's all right. We'll fill in something later. Here, put your name on there, eh?

121

Wagstaff: Gee, I didn't know you could write. Wait a minute, wait a minute! This isn't legal. There's no seal on it. Where's the seal?

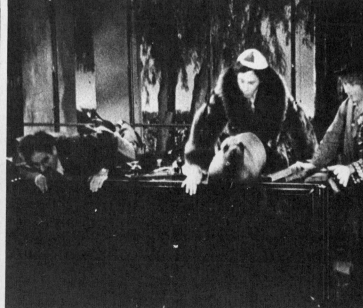

Wagstaff takes his son's love life into his own hands.

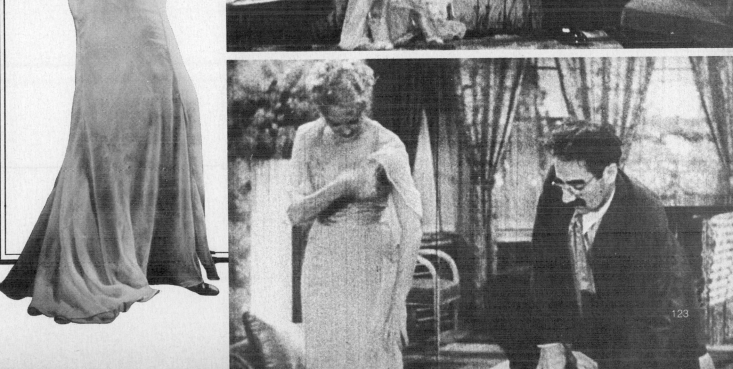

HORSEFEATHERS

Wagstaff: Are you Miss Bailey? Come, come, one of us is Miss Bailey and I'm not.
Connie: I'm Miss Bailey, and who are you?
Wagstaff: I'm Professor Wagstaff. Who are you?

Connie: Miss Bailey.
Wagstaff: Ah, then you **are** Miss Bailey. Thought you could slip one over on me, didn't you? Listen, madame, you've gotta give my son up.

Connie: Give him up?

Wagstaff: You can't take him from me. He's all I've got in the world except a picture of George Washington crossing the Delaware.

Connie: But, Professor, I—

Wagstaff: Whatever you say is a lie. He's only a shell of his former self, which nobody can deny. Whoopee!

Connie: Oh!

Wagstaff: I tell you, you're ruining that boy. You're ruining him. Why can't you do as much for me?

HORSEFEATHERS

Wagstaff: Did my son tell you you had beautiful eyes?
Connie: Why, yes.
Wagstaff: He told me that too. He tells that to everyone he meets.

Wagstaff: Oh, I love sitting on your lap. I could sit here all day if you didn't stand up.

Connie: Quick! Hurry! Get out of here. That door!

Connie: I don't want any ice. Oh!

HORSEFEATHERS

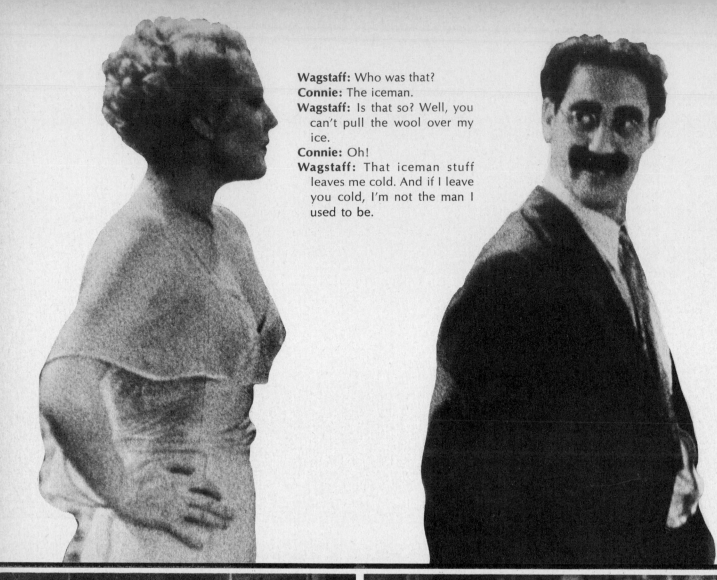

Wagstaff: Who was that?
Connie: The iceman.
Wagstaff: Is that so? Well, you can't pull the wool over my ice.
Connie: Oh!
Wagstaff: That iceman stuff leaves me cold. And if I leave you cold, I'm not the man I used to be.

Frank: Here you are—
Wagstaff: So! I caught you at last. Then you **are** fooling around with this woman. Oh, the shame of it! That I should live to see a son of mine try to take a dame away from his father!

HORSEFEATHERS

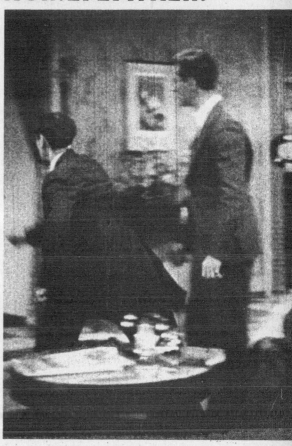

Frank: Dad, I can—
Wagstaff: Enough of this. You leave here immediately and I'll stay here and settle with this woman. And as soon as we're settled, we'll have you over for dinner. On second thought, I'll go with you. Come, follow me.

Wagstaff: There'll always be a lamp in the window for my wandering boy.

HORSEFEATHERS

Wagstaff: Let's see. Where were we? Oh, yes, I was on your lap . . . and doing pretty well as I recall it.

KNOCK! KNOCK!

Connie: Quick! Hurry! Get out! Hurry! And remember, stay under cover.
Wagstaff: You've got more students than the college.

Baravelli: Here, lady, you dropped your ice.

Baravelli: Now, do you want any ice?
Connie: No.
Baravelli: Ah, you are beautiful. Ah, so nice. Una donna bellissima! Un' facia la madonna!
Connie: Baravelli, you overcome me.

Connie: But I don't want any ice. **Baravelli:** Neither do I,

Wagstaff: If he thinks I'm gonna tell him, he's crazy!

Baravelli: All right, but remember it was your idea.
Connie: Oh, no!
Baravelli: Lady, I like you. You've got something, but I don't know what it is.

Huxley College has a chance to win the football game if they can kidnap some members of the opposing team.

Wagstaff: Baravelli, you can fix it for our team to win.

Baravelli: Oh, no, I wanna play.

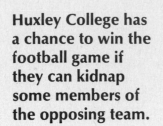

Wagstaff: All right, you can play. But listen, there's two football players on the Darwin team I want kidnapped. Have you ever had any experience as a kidnapper?

Baravelli: You bet. You know what I do when I kidnap somebody? First I call 'em up on the telephone, then I send up my chauffeur.

HORSEFEATHERS

Wagstaff: Oh, have you got a chauffeur?
Baravelli: Yeah.
Wagstaff: What kind of a car have you got?
Baravelli: I no gotta car. I just gotta chauffeur.
Wagstaff: Well, maybe I'm crazy, but when you have a chauffeur, aren't you supposed to have a car?
Baravelli: Well, I had one, but you see, it cost too much money to keep a car and a chauffeur, so I sold the car.

Wagstaff: Well, that shows you how little I know. I would have kept the car and sold the chauffeur.
Baravelli: That'sa no good. I gotta have chauffeur to take me to work in the morning.
Wagstaff: Well, if you've got no car, how can he take you to work?
Baravelli: He don't have to take me to work. I no gotta job.

Wagstaff: Baravelli, this is the finish. How much would you want to stand at the wrong end of a shooting gallery?

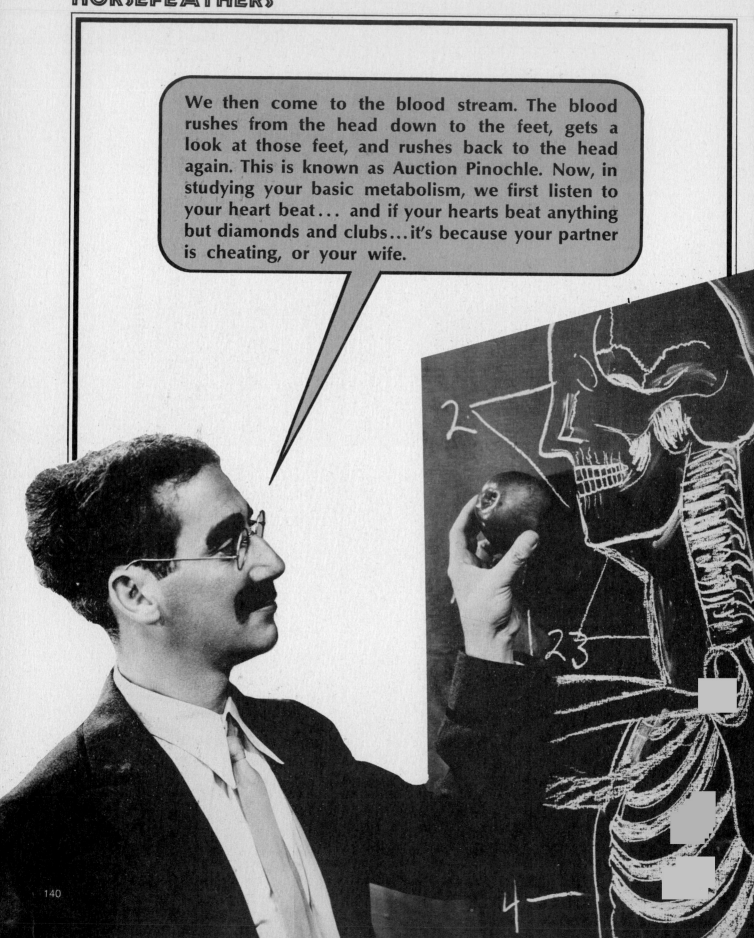

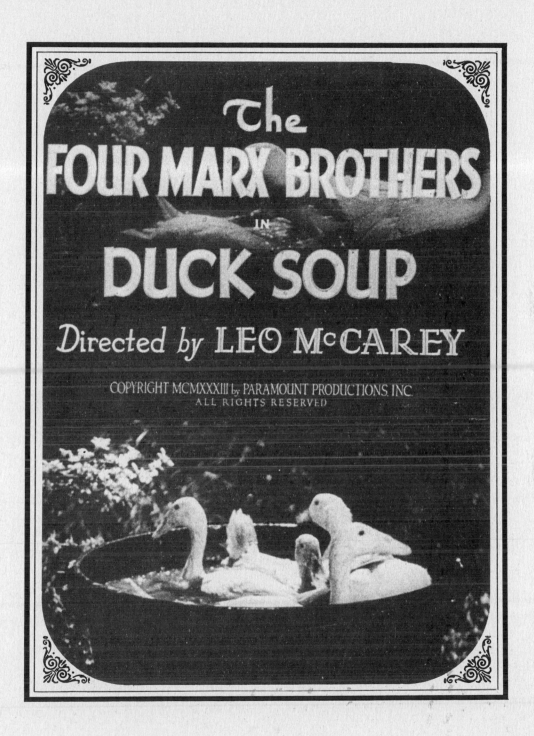

Rufus T. Firefly is named President of Freedonia at the request of Mrs. Teasdale (Margaret Dumont) and it is evident that the country will soon grind to a halt.

Mrs. T (Margaret Dumont): We've been expecting you. As chairwoman of the reception committee, I extend the good wishes of every man, woman and child of Freedonia.
Firefly (Groucho): Never mind that stuff. Take a card.
Mrs. T: A card? What'll I do with a card?
Firefly: You can keep it. I've got fifty-one left. Now, what were you saying?

Mrs. T: As chairwoman of the reception committee, I welcome you with open arms.

Firefly: Is that so? How late do you stay open?

Mrs. T: I've sponsored your appointment because I feel you are the most able statesman in all Freedonia.

Firefly: Well, that covers a lot of ground. Say, you cover a lot of ground yourself. You better beat it. I hear they're going to tear you down and put up an office building where you're standing. You can leave in a taxi. If you can't get a taxi you can leave in a huff. If that's too soon, you can leave in a minute and a huff. You know you haven't stopped talking since I came here? You must have been vaccinated with a phonograph needle.

DUCK SOUP

Mrs. T: The future of Freedonia rests on you. Promise me you'll follow in the footsteps of my husband.

Firefly: How do you like that? I haven't been on the job five minutes and already she's making advances.

Firefly: Not that I care, but where is your husband?
Mrs. T: Why, he's dead.
Firefly: I'll bet he's just using that as an excuse.

Mrs. T: I was with him till the very end.

Firefly: Huh! No wonder he passed away.

Mrs. T: I held him in my arms and kissed him.

Firefly: Oh, I see. Then it was murder. Will you marry me? Did he leave you any money? Answer the second question first.

Mrs. T: He left me his entire fortune.

Firefly: Is that so?

DUCK SOUP

Firefly: Can't you see what I'm trying to tell you? I love you.
Mrs. T: Oh, your Excellency!
Firefly: You're not so bad yourself.
Mrs. T: Oh, I want to present to you Ambassador Trentino of Sylvania. Having him with us today is indeed a great pleasure.

DUCK SOUP

Trentino: Thank you, but I can't stay very long.

Firefly: That's even a greater pleasure. Now, how about lending this country twenty million dollars, you old skinflint?

Trentino: Twenty million dollars is a lot of money. I should have to take that up with my Minister of Finance.

Firefly: Well, in the meantime, could you let me have twelve dollars until pay day?

Trentino: Twelve dollars?

Firefly: Don't be scared. You'll get it back. I'll give you my personal note for ninety days. If it isn't paid by then, you can keep the note.

Trentino: Your Excellency, haven't we seen each other somewhere before?

Firefly: I don't think so. I'm not sure I'm seeing you now. It must be something I ate.

Trentino: Look here, sir, are you trying to—

Firefly: Don't look now, but there's one man too many in this room and I think it's you.

147

ANOTHER LOVE SCENE

Groucho: I could dance with you till the cows come home.

On second thought I'd rather dance with the cows till you came home.

DUCK SOUP

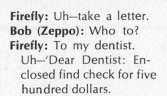

Firefly: Uh—take a letter.
Bob (Zeppo): Who to?
Firefly: To my dentist. Uh—'Dear Dentist: Enclosed find check for five hundred dollars.

Firefly: Yours very truly.' Send that off immediately.
Bob: I'll—uh—I'll have to enclose the check first.
Firefly: You do and I'll fire you.

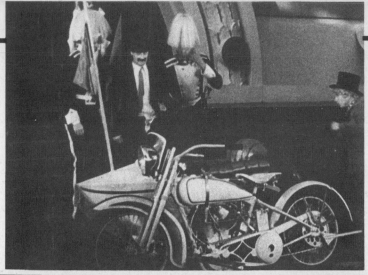

Firefly: I'm in a hurry. To the House of Representatives. Ride like fury. If you run out of gas, get Ethyl. If Ethyl runs out, get Mabel. Now, step on it!

DUCK SOUP

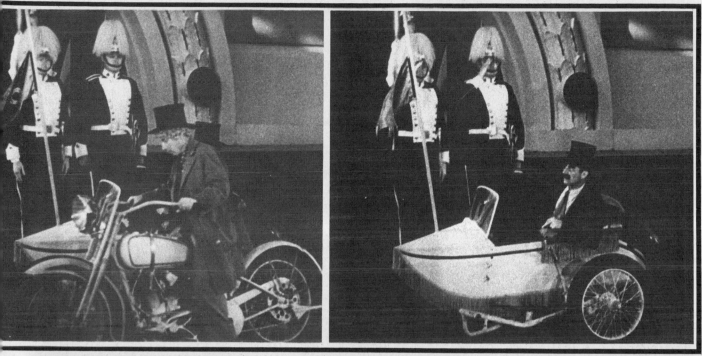

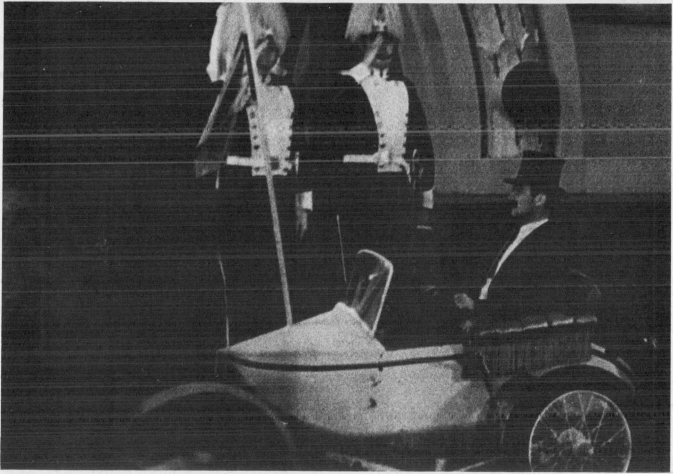

Firefly: Well, it certainly feels good to be back again.

As spies for the rival country of Sylvania, Chicolini (Chico) and Pinky (Harpo) report on Firefly.

Trentino: . . . I want a full detailed report of your investigation.

Chicolini (Chico): All right, I tell you. Monday we watch Firefly's house, but he no come out. He wasn't home. Tuesday we go to the ball game, but he fool us. He no show up. Wednesday he go to the ball game, and we fool him. We no show up. Thursday was a double header. Nobody show up. Friday it rained all day. There was no ball game so we stayed home and we listen to it over the radio.

DUCK SOUP

Trentino: Then you didn't shadow Firefly?
Chicolini: Oh, sure we shadow Firefly. We shadow him all day.

Trentino: But what day was that?   **Chicolini:** Shadderday! 'At'sa some joke, er, Boss?

Trentino: Now, will you tell me, what happened on Saturday?

Chicolini: I'm glad you asked me. We follow this man down to a roadhouse and at this roadhouse he meet a married lady.

Trentino: A married lady?

Chicolini: Yeah. I think it was his wife.

Trentino: Firefly has no wife.

Chicolini: No?

Trentino: No.

Chicolini: Den you know what I think, Boss?

Trentino: What?

Chicolini: I think we follow da wrong man.

DUCK SOUP

A model president presides over a model cabinet meeting to produce the usual results— *nothing.*

Firefly: All right, the meeting is called to order.
Minister of Finance: Your Excellency, here is the Treasury Department's report. I hope you'll find it clear.

DUCK SOUP

Firefly: Clear? Huh! Why, a four-year-old child could understand this report. Run out and find me a four-year-old child. I can't make head or tail out of it.

DUCK SOUP

Firefly: And now, members of the Cabinet —we'll take up old business.
Minister of Commerce: I wish to discuss the tariff.
Firefly: Sit down. That's new business. No old business? Very well—then we'll take up new business.
Minister of Commerce: Now, about that tariff.
Firefly: Too late. That's old business already. Sit down.

Minister of War: Gentlemen, as your Secretary of War, I—

Firefly: The Secretary of War is out of order.

Firefly: Which reminds
me, so is the plumbing.
Make a note of that.
Never mind,
I'll do it myself.

DUCK SOUP

Minister of Labor: The Department of Labor wishes to report that . . . the workers of Freedonia are demanding shorter hours.

Firefly: Very well, we'll give them shorter hours. We'll start by cutting their lunch hour to twenty minutes. And now, gentlemen, we've got to start looking for a new Treasurer.

Minister of Labor: But you appointed one last week. **Firefly:** That's the one I'm looking for.

Minister of War: Gentlemen; Gentlemen! Enough of this. How about taking up the tax?

Firefly: How about taking up the carpet?

Minister of War: I still insist we must take up the tax.

Firefly: He's right. You've got to take up the tacks before you can take up the carpet.

Minister of War: I give all my time and energy to my duties and what do I get?

Firefly: You get awfully tiresome after a while.

Minister of War: Sir, you try my patience!

Firefly: I don't mind if I do. You must come over and try mine some time.

Minister of War: That's the last straw! I resign. I wash my hands of the whole business.

Firefly: A good idea. You can wash your neck, too.

The age-old question of how cabinet members are actually chosen is finally answered.

DUCK SOUP

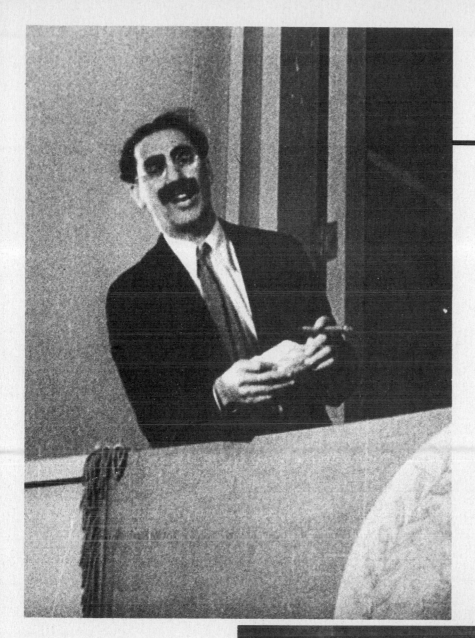

Firefly: Have you got a license?

Chicolini: No, but my dog—he'sa got millions of 'em. Believe me, he's some smart dog. You know, he went with Admiral Byrd to the pole?

Firefly: I'll bet the dog got to the pole first.

Chicolini: You win!

Firefly: Come on up here. I want to scare the Cabinet.

Chicolini: Peanuts:

Firefly: Hey! Do you want to be a public nuisance?

Chicolini: Sure. How much does the job pay?

Firefly: I've got a good mind to join a club and beat you over the head with it.

Chicolini: Peanuts to you!

Chicolini: Hello! No. No. No, he's not in. All right, I'll tell him. Goodbye . . . That was for you.

Firefly: I'm sorry I'm not in. I wanted to have a long talk with you. Now, listen here. You give up that silly peanut stand and I'll get you a soft government job. Now, let's see, what have I got in my Cabinet besides mice? How would you like a job in the mint?

Chicolini: Mint? No, no, I no like-a mint. Uh—what other flavor you got?

Chicolini: Hello, hello. No, not yet. All right, I tell him. Goodbye, thank you. That was for you again.

Firefly: I wonder whatever became of me? I should have been back here a long time ago.

DUCK SOUP

Firefly: Now, listen here. I've got a swell job for you, but first I'll have to ask you a couple of . . . important questions. Now, what is it that has four pair of pants, lives in Philadelphia, and it never rains but it pours?

Chicolini: 'At'sa good one. I give you three guesses.

Firefly: Now, lemme see. Has four pair of pants, lives in Philadelphia. Is it male or female?

Chicolini: No, I no think so.

Firefly: Is he dead?

Chicolini: Who?

Firefly: I don't know. I give up.

Chicolini: I give up, too. Now I ask you another one. What is it got a big black moustache, smokes a big black cigar and is a big pain in the neck.
Firefly: Now, don't tell me. Has a big black moustache, smokes a big black cigar and is a big pain in the—
Chicolini: Uh—

Firefly: Does he wear glasses?
Chicolini: 'At'sa right. You guess it quick.
Firefly: Just for that you don't get the job I was going to give you.
Chicolini: What job?
Firefly: Secretary of War.
Chicolini: All right, I take it.
Firefly: Sold!

Firefly: I've got an appointment to insult Ambassador Trentino and I don't want to keep him waiting. Step on it!

Firefly: This is the fifth trip I've made today and I haven't been anywhere yet.

DUCK SOUP

The Firefly method of diplomacy—instant war.

Trentino: Gloria, I've waited for years. I can't be put off any longer. I love you! I want you! Can't you see I'm at your feet?

Firefly: When you get through with her feet, you can start on mine! If that isn't an insult, I don't know what is!

DUCK SOUP

Firefly: Gloria, I love you! I realize how lonely you are.

Trentino: Can't we go someplace where we can be by ourselves?

Firefly: What can this mug offer you? Wealth and family? I can't give you wealth, but —uh—we can have a little family of our own!

Mrs. T: Oh, Rufus!

Firefly: All I can offer you is a roofus over your head.

Mrs. T: Your Excellency, I really don't know what to say.

Firefly: I wouldn't know what to say either if I was in your place.

Firefly: Maybe you can suggest something. As a matter of fact, you do suggest something. To me you suggest a baboon.

Trentino: What?

Firefly: I—I'm sorry I said that. It isn't fair to the rest of the baboons.

Trentino: This man's conduct is inexcusable. Why, I'll—

Mrs. T: Oh, gentlemen, gentlemen!

Trentino: I did not come here to be insulted!

Mrs. T: Oh!

Firefly: That's what you think!

Trentino: You swine!

Firefly: Come again?

Trentino: You worm!

Firefly: Once more?

Trentino: You upstart!

Firefly: That's it!

Firefly: Touche!

Mrs. T: Oh!

Trentino: Mrs. Teasdale, I'm afraid this regrettable occurrence may plunge our countries into war.

Mrs. T: Oh, this is terrible!

Trentino: I've said enough. I'm a man of few words.

Firefly: I'm a man of one word. Scram! The man doesn't live who can call a Firefly an upstart. Why, the Mayflower was full of Fireflys, and a few horseflies, too. The Fireflys were on the upper deck and the horseflies were on the Fireflys. Good day, my sweet.

Mrs. T: Oh, your Excellency, I must speak to you!

Firefly: I'll see you at the theatre tonight. I'll hold your seat till you get there. After you get there, you're on your own.

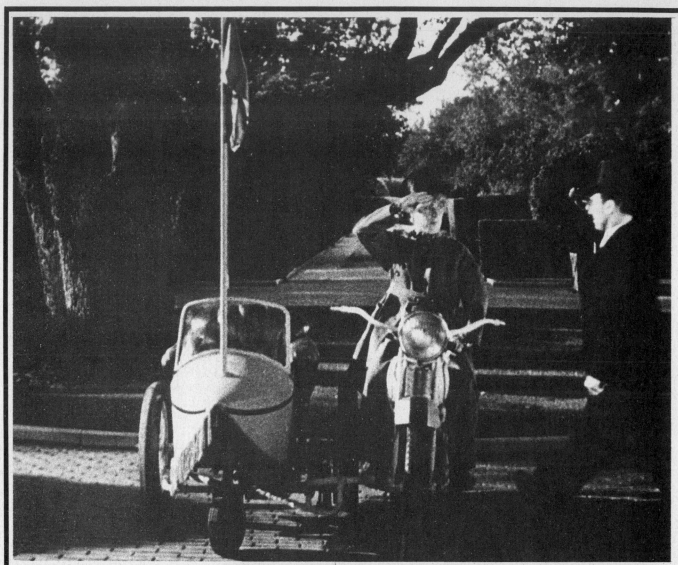

Firefly: His Excellency's car!

DUCK SOUP

Firefly: Oh, no, you don't! I'm not taking any more chances. You can only fool a Firefly twice. This time you ride in the sidecar.

Firefly: This is the only way to travel!

DUCK SOUP

DUCK SOUP

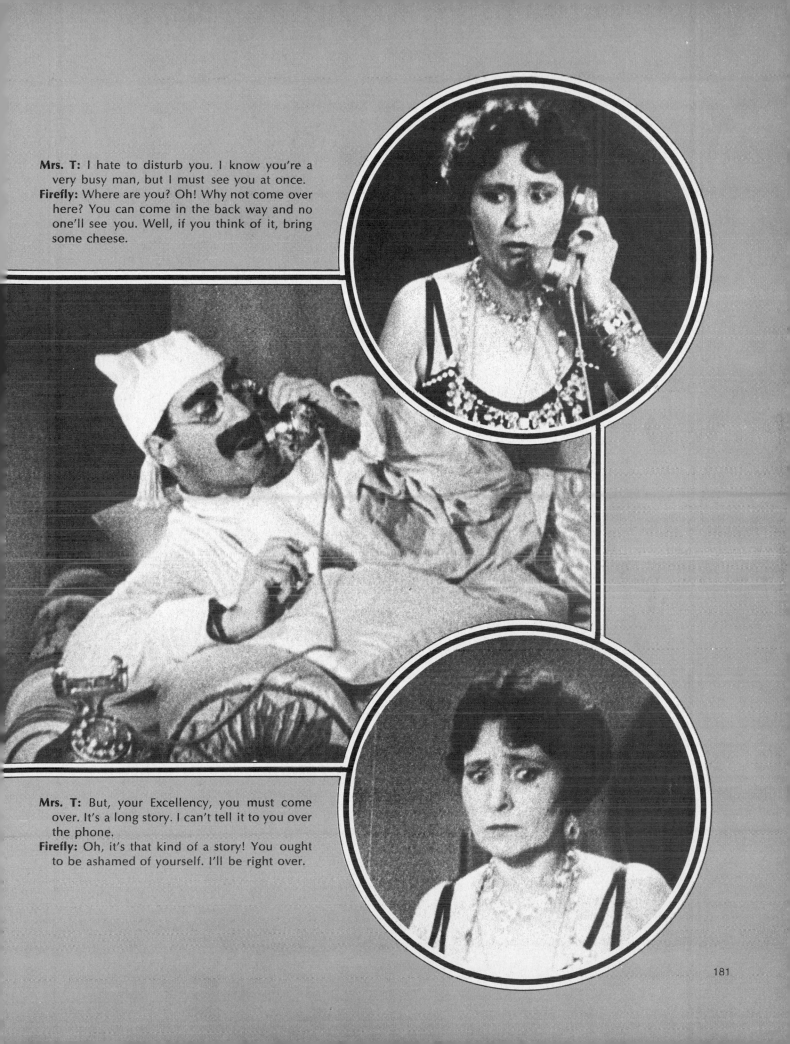

Mrs. T: I hate to disturb you. I know you're a very busy man, but I must see you at once.
Firefly: Where are you? Oh! Why not come over here? You can come in the back way and no one'll see you. Well, if you think of it, bring some cheese.

Mrs. T: But, your Excellency, you must come over. It's a long story. I can't tell it to you over the phone.
Firefly: Oh, it's that kind of a story! You ought to be ashamed of yourself. I'll be right over.

181

Firefly: After I leave here tonight, will you ever forgive me? Here are the plans of war. They're as valuable as your life, and that's putting 'em pretty cheap. Watch them like a cat watches her kittens. Have you ever had kittens? No, of course not. You're too busy running around playing bridge. Can't you see what I'm trying to tell you?

Firefly: I love you. Why don't you marry me?
Mrs. T: Why, marry you?
Firefly: You take me and I'll take a vacation. I'll need a vacation if we're going to get married. Married! I can see you right now in the kitchen, bending over a hot stove, but I can't see the stove. Come, come, say the word and you'll never see . . .

Firefly: . . . me again. Gloria!

Mrs. T: Rufus, what are you thinking of?

Firefly: Oh, I was just thinking of all the years I wasted collecting stamps. Oh—uh—I suppose you'll think me a sentimental old fluff, but—uh—would you mind giving me a lock of your hair?

Mrs. T: A lock of my hair? Why, I had no idea.

Firefly: I'm letting you off easy. I was going to ask for the whole wig.

DUCK SOUP

Firefly: Lieutenant, why weren't the original indictment papers placed in my portfolio?

Bob: Why—uh—I didn't think those papers were important at this time, your Excellency.

Firefly: You didn't think they were important? You realize I had my dessert wrapped in those papers? Here, take this bottle back and get two cents for it.

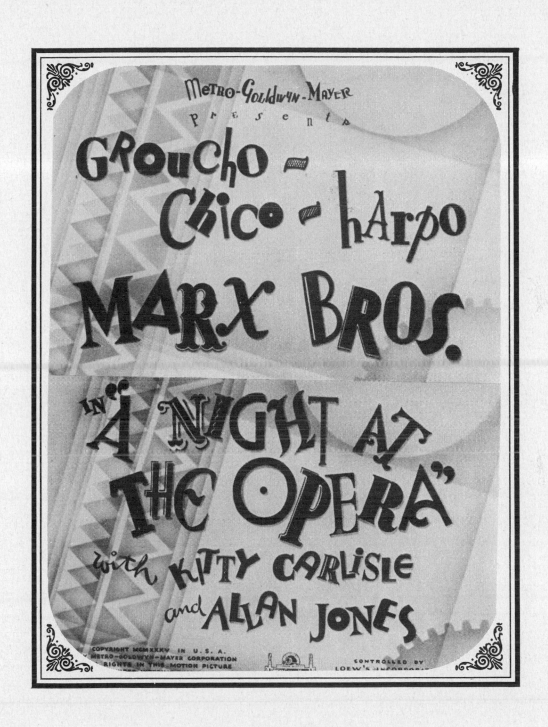

Groucho has promised Margaret Dumont that he would get her into society —so far he hasn't even shown up for dinner.

Mrs. Claypool (Margaret Dumont): Oh, boy!
Bellboy: Yes, Madame?
Mrs. Claypool: Will you page Mr. Otis B. Driftwood, please? Mr. Otis B. Driftwood.

Bellboy: Paging Mr. Driftwood. Mr. Driftwood. Mr. Driftwood. Mr. Driftwood.

Driftwood: (Groucho Marx) Boy!

Driftwood: Will you do me a favor and stop yelling my name all over this restaurant? Do I go 'round yelling your name?

A NIGHT AT THE OPERA

Mrs. Claypool: Mr. Driftwood

Driftwood: Say, is your voice changing, or is somebody else paging me around here?

Mrs. Claypool: Mr. Driftwood

Driftwood: Why, Mrs. Claypool! Hello!

Mrs. Claypool: Mr. Driftwood, you invited me to dine with you at seven o'clock. It is now eight o'clock, and no dinner.

Driftwood: What do you mean, no dinner? I just had one of the biggest meals I ever ate in my life, and no thanks to you, either.

Mrs. Claypool: I've been sitting right here since seven o'clock.

Driftwood: Yes, with your back to me. When I invite a woman to dinner, I expect her to look at my face. That's the price she has to pay.

A NIGHT AT THE OPERA

Waiter: Your check, sir.

Driftwood: Nine dollars and forty cents! This is an outrage! If I were you, I wouldn't pay it.

Driftwood: Now then, Mrs. Claypool, what are we going to have for dinner?

Mrs. Claypool: You've had your dinner.

Driftwood: All right, we'll have breakfast. Waiter!

Waiter: Yes, sir.

Driftwood: Have you—got any milk fed chicken?

Waiter: Yes, sir.

Driftwood: Well, squeeze the milk out of one and bring me a glass.

Waiter: Yes, sir.

Mrs. Claypool: Mr. Driftwood, three months ago you promised to put me into society. In all that time, you've done nothing but draw a very handsome salary.

Driftwood: You think that's nothing, huh? How many men do you suppose are drawing a handsome salary nowadays? Why, you can count them on the fingers of one hand, my good woman.

Mrs. Claypool: I'm not your good woman!

A NIGHT AT THE OPERA

Driftwood: Don't say that, Mrs. Claypool. I don't care what your past has been. To me, you'll always be my good woman, because I love you. There, I didn't mean to tell you, but you, you dragged it out of me. I love you.

Mrs. Claypool: It's rather difficult to believe that when I find you dining with another woman.

Driftwood: That woman? Do you know why I sat with her?

Mrs. Claypool: No—

Driftwood: Because she reminded me of you.

Mrs. Claypool: Really?

Driftwood: Of course! That's why I'm sitting here with you, because you remind me of you. Your eyes, your throat, your lips, everything about you reminds me of you, except you. How do you account for that? If she figures that one out, she's good.

Mrs. Claypool: Mr. Driftwood, I think we'd better keep everything on a business basis.

Driftwood: How do you like that? Everytime I get romantic with you, you want to talk business. I don't know, there's something about me that brings out the business in every woman.

A NIGHT AT THE OPERA

Driftwood: All right, we'll talk business. You see that man over there... eating spaghetti?

Mrs. Claypool: No.

Driftwood: Well, you. . . . see the spaghetti, don't you? Now, behind that spaghetti is none other than Herman Gottlieb, Director of the New York Opera Company. Do you follow me?

Mrs. Claypool: Yes.

Driftwood: Well, stop followin' me, or I'll have you arrested. Now, I've arranged for you to invest two hundred thousand dollars in the New York Opera Company.

Mrs. Claypool: I don't understand.

Driftwood: Don't you see? You'll be a patron of the opera. You'll get into society. Then you can marry me and they'll kick you out of society. And all you've lost is two hundred thousand dollars.

Gottlieb: Ah. Mr. . . . Driftwood!

Driftwood: Ah, Gottlieb. Allow me. Mrs. Claypool, Mr. Gottlieb. Mr. Gottlieb, Mrs. Claypool. Mrs. Claypool. Mrs. Claypool, M-- I could go on like this all night, but it's tough on my suspenders. Now, where was I? Oh yes! Mrs. Claypool, Mr. Gottlieb, Mr. Gottlieb, Mrs. Claypool. Mrs. Claypool, Mr. Gottlieb. Mr. Gottlieb, Mrs. Claypool—

Driftwood: Now, if you four people want to play bridge, don't mind me. Go right ahead.
Gottlieb: Mrs. Claypool, I am so happy.

Mrs. Claypool: What are you doing?

Driftwood: I just wanted to see if your rings were still there.

A NIGHT AT THE OPERA

Chico claims to be the manager for a tenor whom Groucho would like to sign as singer with the New York Opera Company. Now that they have found each other all that is necessary to complete their little deal is a simple contract.

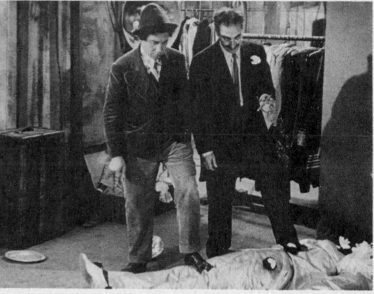

> **Forelo:** What's the matter, mister?
> **Driftwood:** Oh, we had an argument and he pulled a knife on me, so I shot him.
> **Forelo:** Do you mind if I—
> **Driftwood:** No, no, go right ahead. Plenty of room.

Driftwood: Two beers, bartender.
Forelo: I'll take two beers, too.

Driftwood: Well, things seem to be getting better around the country.

Forelo: I don't know. I'm a stranger here myself.
Driftwood: Say, I just remembered. I came back here looking for somebody. You don't know who it is, do you?

Forelo: It's a funny thing. It just slipped my mind.
Driftwood: Oh, I know—I know.

The greatest tenor in the world—that's what I'm after.
Forelo: Well, I'm his manager.

Driftwood: Whose manager?
Forelo: The greatest tenor in the world.

Driftwood: The fellow that sings at the opera here?
Forelo: Sure.

Driftwood: What's his name?

Forelo: What do you care? I can't pronounce it. What do you want with him?

Driftwood: Well—uh—I want to sign him up for the New York Opera Company. Do you know that America is waiting to hear him sing?

Forelo: Well, he can sing loud, but he can't sing that loud.

Driftwood: Well, I think I can get America to meet him halfway. Could he sail tomorrow?

Forelo: You pay him enough money he could sail yesterday. How much you pay him?

Driftwood: Well, I don't know.

Driftwood: Let's see—a thousand dollars a night. I'm entitled to a small profit. How about ten dollars a night?

Forelo: Ten—ten dollars! I'll take it.

Driftwood: All right, but remember, I get ten per cent for negotiating the deal.

A NIGHT AT THE OPERA

Forelo: Yes, and I get ten per cent for being the manager. How much does that leave?

Driftwood: Well, that leaves him—uh—eight dollars.

Forelo: Eight dollars, eh? Well, he sends a five dollars home to his mother.

Driftwood: Well, that leaves three dollars.

Forelo: Three dollars. Can he live in New York on three dollars?

Driftwood: Like a prince. Of course, he won't be able to eat, but he can live like a prince. However, out of that three dollars, you know, he'll have to pay an income tax.

Forelo: Oh, his income tax, eh?

Driftwood: Yes. You know, there's a Federal tax and a State tax and a city tax and a street tax and a sewer tax.

Forelo: How much does this come to?

Driftwood: Well, I figure if he doesn't sing too often he can break even.

Forelo: All right, we take it.

Driftwood: All right, fine. Now—uh—here are the contracts. You just put his name at the top and—uh—and you sign at the bottom. There's no need of you reading that because these are duplicates.

Forelo: Yes, duplicates. Duplicates, eh?

Driftwood: All right. I'll read it to you.

Driftwood: Can you hear?

Forelo: I haven't heard anything yet.

Forelo: Did you say anything?

Driftwood: Well, I haven't said anything worth hearing.

Driftwood: Well, I wouldn't know about that. I haven't been in Canada in years. Well, go ahead and read it.

Forelo: What does it say?

Driftwood: Well, go on and read it.

Forelo: All right—you read it.

Driftwood: I say, they're—they're duplicates.

Forelo: Oh, sure, it's a duplicate. Certainly.

Driftwood: Don't you know what duplicates are?

Forelo: Sure. Those five kids up in Canada.

Forelo: Well, that's why I didn't hear anything.

Driftwood: Well, that's why I didn't say anything.

Forelo: Can you read?

Driftwood: I can read but I can't see it. I don't séem . . . to have it

A NIGHT AT THE OPERA

Forelo: Uh—just the first part.

Driftwood: What do you mean? The—the party of the first part?

Forelo: No, the first part of the party of the first part.

in focus here. If my arms were a little longer, I could read it. You haven't got a baboon in your pocket have you? Here—here—here we are. Now, I've got it. Now, pay particular attention to this first clause because it's most important. Says the —uh—the party of the first part shall be known in this contract as the party of the first part. How do you like that? That's pretty neat, eh?

Forelo: No, that's no good.

Driftwood: What's the matter with it?

Forelo: I don't know. Let's hear it again.

Driftwood: Says the—uh—the party of the first part should be known in this contract as the party of the first part.

Forelo: That sounds a little better this time.

Driftwood: Well, it grows on you. Would you like to hear it once more?

Driftwood: All right. It says the—uh—the first part of the party of the first part, should be known in this contract as the first part of the party of the first part, should be known in this contract — look. Why should we quarrel about a thing like this? We'll take it right out, eh?

A NIGHT AT THE OPERA

Forelo: Yeah. It's too long anyhow. Now, what have we got left?

Driftwood: Well, I've got about a foot and a half.

Now, it says—uh—the party of the second part shall be known in this contract as the party of the second part.

Forelo: Hey, look! Why can't the first part of the second party be the second part of the first party? Then you've got something.

Driftwood: Well, look—uh—rather than go through all that again, what do you say?

Forelo: Fine.

Driftwood: Now—uh—now, I've got something here you're bound to like. You'll be crazy about it.

Forelo: No, I don't like it.

Driftwood: You don't like what?

Forelo: Whatever it is—I don't like it.

Forelo: Well, I don't know about that.
Driftwood: Now, what's the matter?
Forelo: I no like the second party either.

Driftwood: Well, you should have come to the first party. We didn't get home till around four in the morning. I was blind for three days.

Driftwood: Well, don't let's break up an old friendship over a thing like that. Ready?

Forelo: Okay. Now, the next part, I don't think you're going to like.

Driftwood: Well, your word's good enough for me. Now, then, is my word good enough for you?

Forelo: I should say not.

Driftwood: Well, that takes out two more clauses.

Driftwood: Now the party of the eighth part—
Forelo: No.

Driftwood: No?
Forelo: No. That's no good. No.

Driftwood: The party of the ninth—
Forelo: No, that's no good too.

Forelo: Hey, how is it my contract is skinnier than yours?
Driftwood: Well, I don't know. You must have been out on a tear last night. But, anyhow, we're all set now, aren't we?

A NIGHT AT THE OPERA

Driftwood: Now, just—uh—just you put your name right down there and then the deal is—is—uh—legal.

Forelo: I forgot to tell you. I can't write.

Driftwood: Well, that's all right. There's no ink in the pen anyhow. But, listen, it's a contract, isn't it?

Forelo: Oh, sure.

Forelo: Hey, wait—wait! What does this say here? This thing here?

Driftwood: Oh, that? Oh, that's the usual clause. That's in every contract. That just says—uh—it says—uh—if any of the parties participating in this contract is shown not to be in their right mind, the entire agreement is automatically nullified.

Forelo: Well, I don't know.

Driftwood: It's all right. That's—that's in every contract. That's—that's what they call a sanity clause.

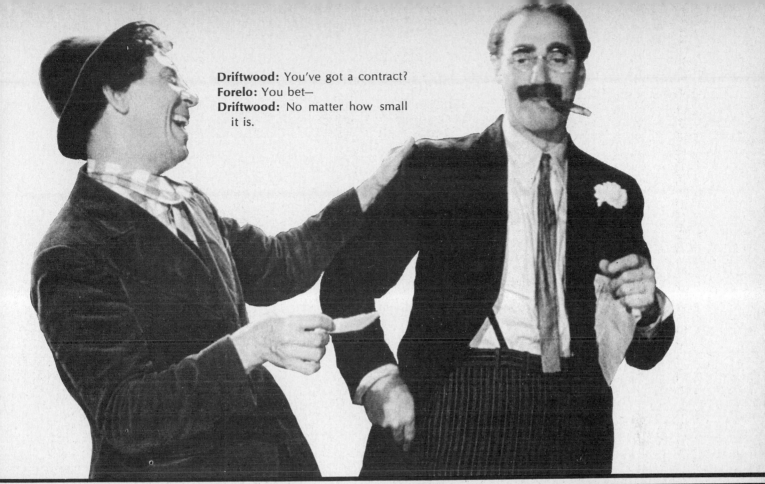

Driftwood: You've got a contract?
Forelo: You bet—
Driftwood: No matter how small it is.

Driftwood: Well, you win the white . . . carnation. Sanity Claus.

A NIGHT AT THE OPERA

With the New York Opera Company picking up the tab, Otis Driftwood sets sail from Europe to New York. Once on board Driftwood learns that his stateroom is no bigger than a breadbox and on top of it all he finds three stowaways in his trunk . . . Chico, Harpo & Allan Jones.

Driftwood: Hey, what's the idea? Hit and run driver, eh? **Steward:** I—I'm sorry, sir.

Driftwood: Sorry, my eye. Look at that fender. It's all bumped out of shape. You'll pay for this, my good man. Let me see your number? Thirty-two. eh?

Driftwood: Have you got any insurance?
Steward: What?
Driftwood: Are you insured?
Steward: No, sir.

Driftwood: Well, you're just the fellow I want to see. I have here an accident policy that will absolutely protect you—no matter what happens. If you lose a leg, we'll help you look for it and all this will cost you is—uh—what have you got there? One dollar? Here you are.

All right, let's go. Suite fifty-eight and don't go over twenty miles an hour.

A NIGHT AT THE OPERA

Driftwood: Ah. Hello, Toots.
Mrs. Claypool: Hello.
Driftwood: Say, pretty classy layout you have here.
Mrs. Claypool: Do you like it?
Driftwood: Ah, twin beds. You little rascal, you!
Mrs. Claypool: One of those is a day bed.
Driftwood: A likely story. Have you read any good books lately?

Mrs. Claypool: Mr. Driftwood . . . would you please get off the bed? What would people say?

Driftwood: They'd probably say you're a very lucky woman. Now will you please shut up so I can continue my reading?

Mrs. Claypool: No. I will not shut up. And will you kindly get up at once?

Driftwood: All right, I'll go. I'll make you another proposition. Let's go in my room and talk the situation over.

Mrs. Claypool: What situation?

Driftwood: Well—uh—what situations have you got?

Mrs. Claypool: I will most certainly not go to your room.

Driftwood: Okay, then I'll stay here!

Mrs. Claypool: All right. All right. I'll come, but get out.

Driftwood: Shall we say—uh—ten minutes?

Mrs. Claypool: Yes, ten minutes—anything—but go!

Driftwood: Because if you're not there in ten minutes, I'll be back here in eleven—with squeaky shoes on.

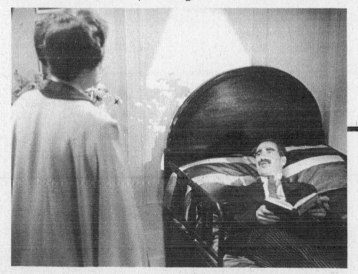

A NIGHT AT THE OPERA

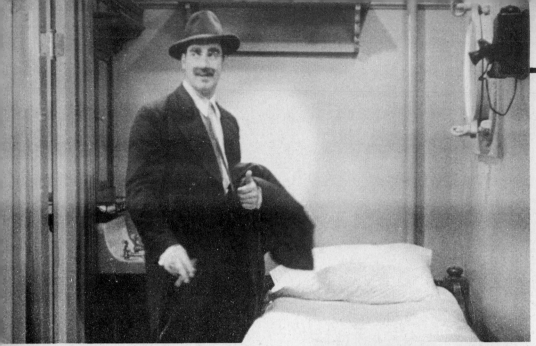

A NIGHT AT THE OPERA

Driftwood: Hey, wait a minute! Wait a minute! This can't be my room!

Steward: Yes, sir, suite number fifty-eight, sir.

Driftwood: Fifty-eight? That's an awful big number for a birdcage this size. Wouldn't it be simpler if you put the stateroom in the trunk? Say, who was responsible for installing me in this telephone booth?

Steward: Mr. Gottlieb picked it out for you, sir.

Driftwood: Gottlieb, eh? Well, that's awfully decent of him, awfully decent. Did he pick out the whole room or just the porthole?

Steward: I'm sure you'll find it very cozy, sir.

Driftwood: Cozy? Cozy is hardly the word for it.

Steward: Anything else, sir?

Driftwood: Yes. Tomorrow you can take the trunk out and I'll go in.

Driftwood: Sing, Ho! For the open highway. Sing, Ho! For the open—
Chico: Hello, boss. What are you doing here?
A. Jones: Hello.
Driftwood: Well, this makes it a perfect voyage. I'm terribly sorry, but I thought this was my trunk.
Chico: This is your trunk.
Driftwood: I don't remember packing you boys. Well, we're still in the harbor. As soon as we get out in the open ocean, there'll be plenty of room.
Chico: Yeah, sure.

Driftwood: Hey, isn't that my shirt you're wearing?
Chico: Hey, look out—I don't know. I found it in the trunk.
Driftwood: Well, then it couldn't be mine. Well, it's nice seeing you boys, but I was expecting my other suit. You didn't happen to see it, did you?
Chico: Yeah, it took up too much room, so we sold it.
Driftwood: Did you get anything for it?
Chico: A dollar forty.
Driftwood: That's my suit all right. It's lucky I left another shirt in the drawer.

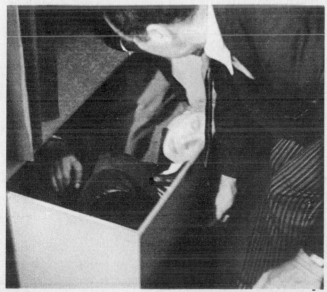

Driftwood: This can't be my shirt. My shirt doesn't snore!
Chico: Shh. Don't wake him up. He's got insomnia —he's trying to sleep it off.
Driftwood: That's as grizzly a looking object as I've ever seen. Well, get him up out of there.

Driftwood: Well, I wish you fellows would explain this thing to me.
Chico: Well, itssa very simple. You see, Ricardo, he's in love with Rosa. Rosa, she go to New York. We want to go to New York too, but we gotta no money, so we hide in the trunk.

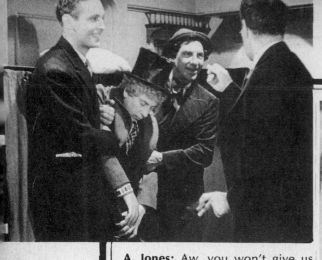

A. Jones: Aw, you won't give us away, will you, Mr. Driftwood?

Driftwood: No, but you fellows have got to get out of here. I've got a date with a lady in a few minutes and you know the old saying, 'two's company and five's a crowd.'

Chico: We go, but first we want something to eat. We no eat all day. We're hungry.

Driftwood: We'll discuss the food situation later.

Chico: We get food or we don't go.

Driftwood: I knew I never should have met you fellows. All right, but you've got to promise to scram out as soon as you've eaten.

Chico: All right.

Driftwood: I'll go get the Steward and you fellows be quiet. Remember you're stowaways.

Chico: All right. We say nothin'.

Driftwood: All right. Now just put that bag of jello over here. Wouldn't it be simpler if you just had him stuffed?

Chico: He's no olive.

Driftwood: I'll go get the steward. Say, is this the door of the room or am I in the trunk?

Steward: Yes, sir?

Driftwood: I say, stew—

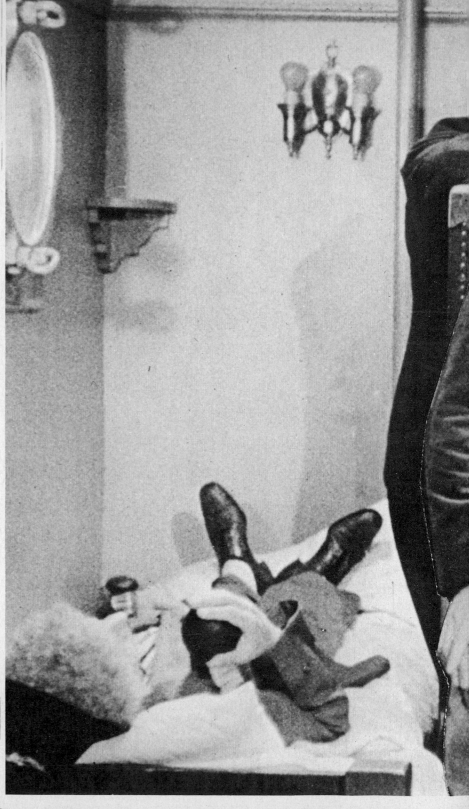

A NIGHT AT THE OPERA

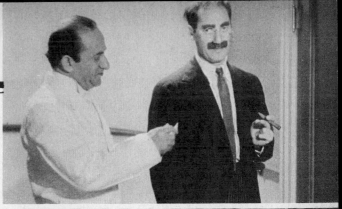

Steward: Yes, sir?

Driftwood: What have we got for dinner?

Steward: Anything you like, sir. You might have some tomato juice, orange juice, grape juice, pineapple juice—

Driftwood: Hey, turn off the juice before I get electrocuted. All right, let me have one of each. And two fried eggs, two poached eggs, two scrambled eggs and two medium boiled eggs.

Chico: And two hard boiled eggs.

Driftwood: And two hard boiled eggs.

Harpo: Honk!

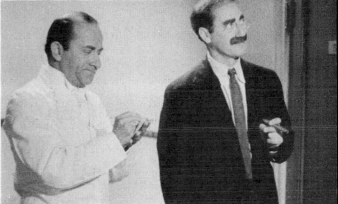

Driftwood: Make that **three** hard boiled eggs. And some Roast Beef—rare, medium, well done and over done.

Chico: And two hard boiled eggs!

Driftwood: And two hard boiled eggs.

Harpo: Honk! Honk!

Driftwood: Make that three hard boiled eggs and one duck egg. Have you got any stewed prunes

Steward: Yes, sir.

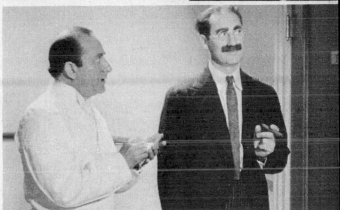

Driftwood: Well, give them some black coffee, that'll sober them up!

Chico: And two hard boiled eggs!

Driftwood: And two hard boiled eggs.

Harpo: Honk! Honk! Honk! Honk! Honk! Honk! Honk!

Driftwood: It's either foggy out or make that twelve more hard boiled eggs. And steward, rush that order because the faster it comes, the faster this convention will be over.

Steward: Yes, sir.

Driftwood: Do they allow tipping on the boat?

Steward: Oh, yes sir!

Driftwood: Have you got two fives?

Steward: Yes, sir!

Driftwood: Well, then you won't need the ten cents I was going to give you.

15

Driftwood: Well, that's fine. If the Steward is deaf and dumb, he'll never know you're in here.
Chico: Oh, sure—that's all right.
Driftwood: Yes.
Maid: We've come to make up your room.
Chico: Are those my hard boiled eggs?

Driftwood: I can't tell until they get into the room. Come on in girls and leave all hope behind. But you've got to work fast because you've got to be out in ten minutes.

A NIGHT AT THE OPERA

Driftwood: Hey, there's a slight misunderstanding here. I said the girls had to work fast, not your friend!

Chico: He's still asleep.

Driftwood: You know he does better asleep than I do awake! YES!

Engineer: I'm the engineer. I came to turn off the heat.

Driftwood: Well, you can start right in on him.

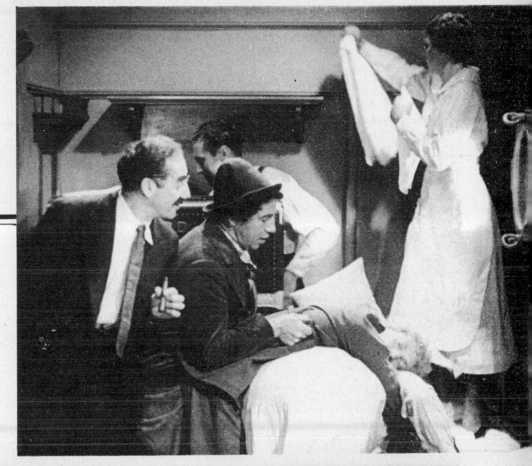

Driftwood: YES!
Manicurist: Did you want a manicure?
Driftwood: No. Come on in. I hadn't planned on a manicure, but I think on a journey like this you ought to have every convenience you <u>can</u> get.

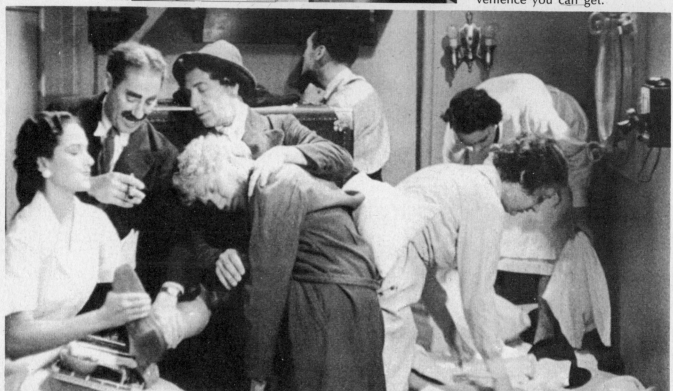

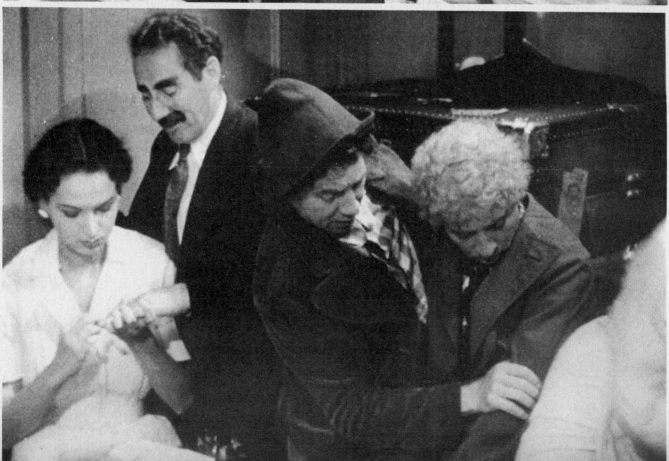

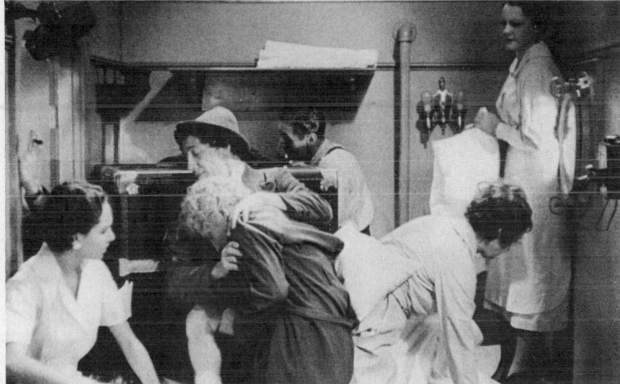

Engineer's Ass't: I'm the Engineer's assistant.

Driftwood: You know, I had a premonition you were going to show up.

A NIGHT AT THE OPERA

Driftwood: The Engineer is right over in the corner. You can chop your way right through. Say, is it my imagination, or is it getting crowded in here?
Chico: Oh, I've got plenty of room.

Girl: Is my Aunt Minnie in here?
Driftwood: Well, you can come in and prowl around if you want to. If she isn't in here you could probably find someone just as good.
Girl: Well, could I use your phone?
Driftwood: Use the phone? I'll lay you even money you can't get in the room! We're liable to be in New York before you can get to that phone.

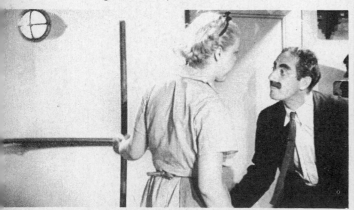

Washwoman: I came to mop up.
Driftwood: Just the woman I'm looking for. Come right ahead!

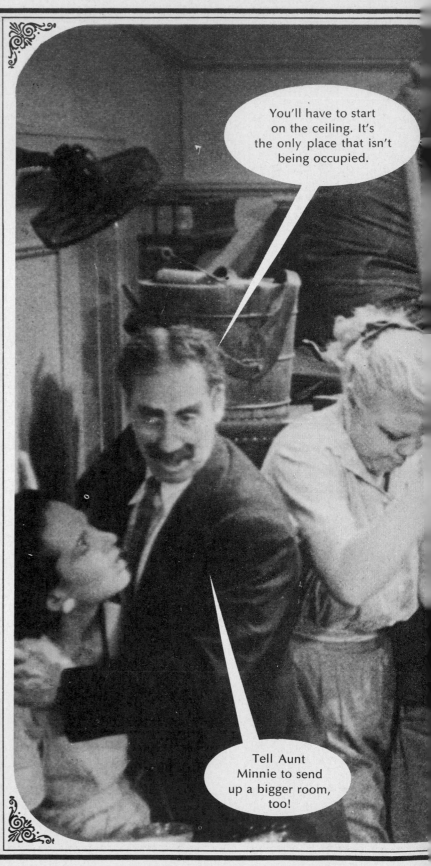

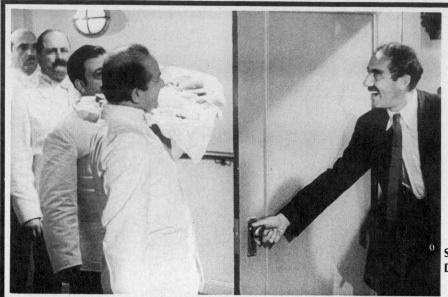

Steward: Stewards!
Driftwood: Ah, come right ahead!

A NIGHT AT THE OPERA

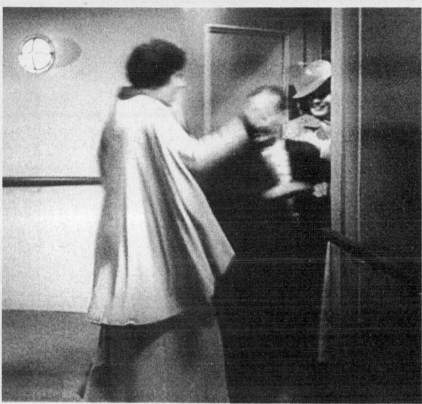

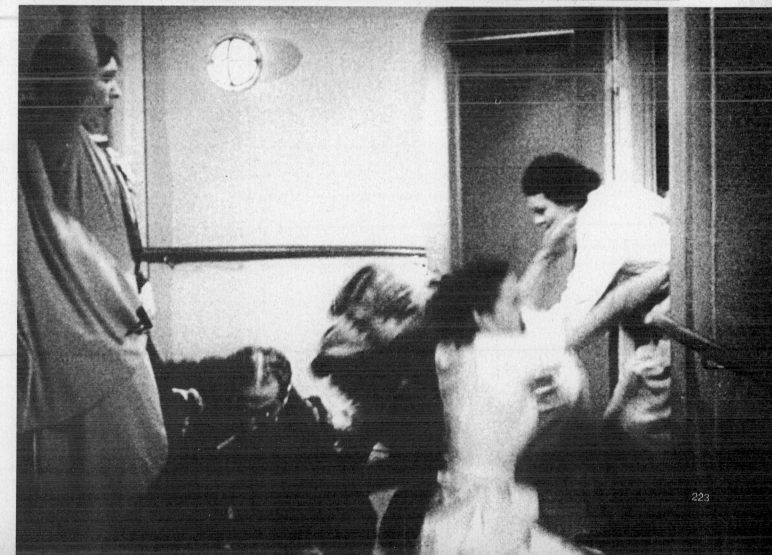

The problem: how to get three stowaways into the country. Solution: dress them as famed Russian aviators and get them a public welcome to the City of New York.

Mayor: And so, my friends, as Mayor of this great city, I take pleasure in inviting our distinguished visitors to tell us something about their achievements.

Forelo (Chico Marx): What'll I say?
Driftwood (Groucho Marx): Tell 'em you're not here.
Forelo: Suppose they don't believe me?
Driftwood: They'll believe you when you start talkin'.

A NIGHT AT THE OPERA

Forelo: Friends—

Driftwood: Talk fast. I see a man in the crowd with a rope.

Forelo: How we happen to come to America is a great story, but I no tell that.

Forelo: When we first started out, we gotta idea you give us this grand reception. We don't deserve it. And when I say we don't deserve it, believe me I know what I'm a-talkin' about. Eh?

Driftwood: That's a novelty.

Forelo: So now I tell you how we fly to America.

Forelo: The first time-a we start-a, we get-a a half way across when we run out of gasoline and we gotta go back. Then I take-a twice as much-a gasoline. This time we were just about to land, maybe three feet, when what do you think? We run out of gasoline again. Then back we go again and get-a more gas. This time I take-a plenty gas.

Forelo: Wella we getta half way over . . . when what do you thinka happen? We forgota the airplane. So we gotta sit down and we talk it over. Then I getta the great idea. We no taka gasoline. We no taka the airplane. We taka steamship. And that, friends . . . is how we fly across the ocean.

Driftwood: I'm going out and arrange your bail.

Mayor: This is the Mayor again. And now I take great pleasure in introducing another of our heroes, who will tell you something of his exploits. Of course.

Driftwood: From now on, it's every man for himself.
Mayor: I would suggest you make your speech a little more direct than your brother's.

Driftwood: What'll you give me to set fire to your beard?

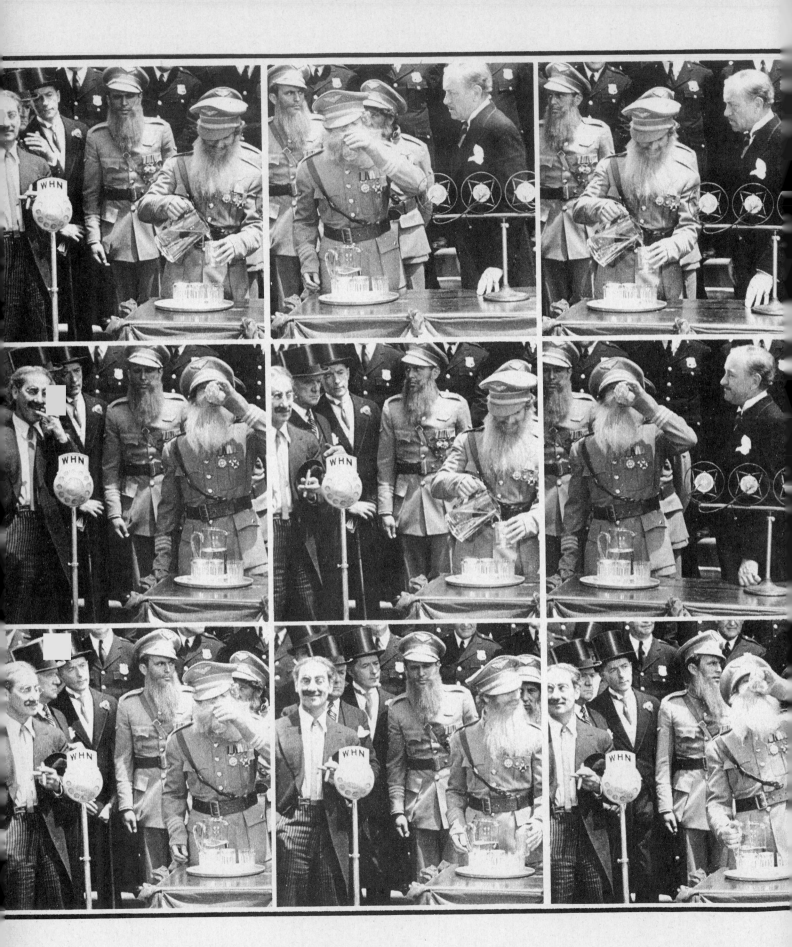

Driftwood: Well, we're all right as long as the water supply holds out.

Mayor: Please — the radio. Your speech!

Driftwood: You know, they may have to build a dam in back of him.

A NIGHT AT THE OPERA

Henderson: Hey, I think these fellows are phonies.

Driftwood: What's that you say?
Henderson: You heard me.
Driftwood: Do you hear what they say? They say they've never been so insulted in their life, and they absolutely refuse to stay here.

Mayor: No, no, please. He didn't mean it. Tell them he didn't mean it.

Driftwood: Of course, you know this means war.

Mayor: Now see what you've done!

Henderson: I'm sorry. I'm awful sorry. I apologize, and I hope you're not offended.

HERE ARE THE THREE STOWAW...
WHO FOOLED CITY HALL!

Scene at the City Hall, when the Mayor presented the key to the city to the supposed Santopoulos Brothers.

232

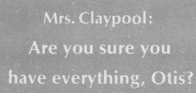

Mrs. Claypool:
Are you sure you
have everything, Otis?

Driftwood:
I've never had any
complaints
yet!

A NIGHT AT THE OPERA

Driftwood: Is the opera
over yet?

Doorman: Not yet, signor.
In a few minutes.

Driftwood: Hey you! I told you to slow that nag down.
On account of you I almost heard the opera! Now then,
once around the park and drive slowly.

A NIGHT AT THE OPERA

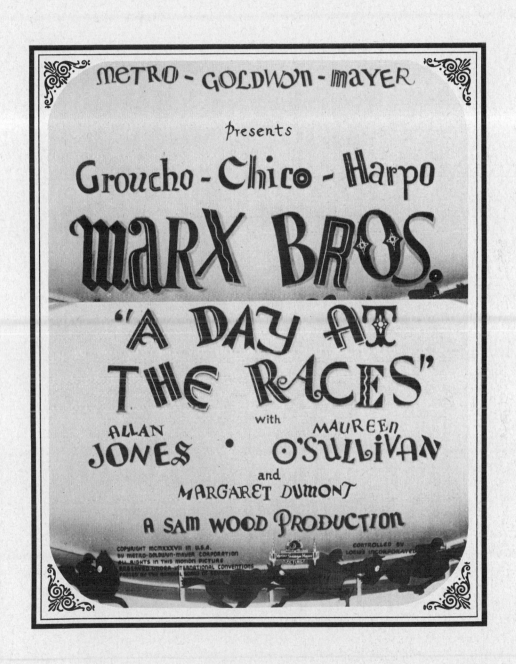

Gil:
Are you a man or a mouse?

Hackenbush:
You put a piece of cheese down here and you'll find out.

A DAY AT THE RACES

Groucho as Dr. Hackenbush, actually a horse doctor, has been summoned by Mrs. Upjohn (Margaret Dumont) to head the Standish Sanitarium.

Mrs. Upjohn (Margaret Dumont): Oh, doctor!
Hackenbush (Groucho): Here, boy. Here, boy . . .
Hackenbush: . . . take these bags and run up to my room. And here's a dime for yourself.·
Mrs. Upjohn: Oh, no, no, no, no, no! This is Mr. Whitmore, our business manager.
Hackenbush: Oh, I'm terribly sorry. Here's a quarter.

Mrs. Upjohn: Oh! You mustn't take the doctor too seriously. He probably feels tired after his long trip.

Hackenbush: Why shouldn't I be tired? ever ride four on a motorcycle? And me—top man!

Mrs. Upjohn: Oh, this is Dr. Hugo Z. Hackenbush, your new Chief of Staff. And now, Doctor, I'd like you to meet Miss Standish. Oh, Doctor . . .

Hackenbush: Just a moment, till I calm these paralytics.

Mrs. Upjohn: Oh, dear. Oh, Doctor . . . Oh, Doctor, this is Miss Standish . . .

Mrs. Upjohn: Now, Doctor, I'd like you to meet your new associates. **1st Doctor:** Johnson, Bellevue Hospital, 1918.

Mrs. Upjohn: Owner of the sanitarium.
Hackenbush: Oh, how do you do, Miss Standish?
Judy: How do you do.
Hackenbush: You're the prettiest owner of a sanitarium I've ever seen.
Judy: Thank you.

Hackenbush: You have a charming place here. Ah, I knew your mother very well. I'll let you in on a little secret. Many, many years ago in the dear dim past, I proposed to your mother.
Judy: Oh, but that's my father.
Hackenbush: No wonder he turned me down.

2nd Doctor: Franko, Johns Hopkins, '22. **3rd Doctor:** Wilmerding, Mayo Bros., '24. **Hackenbush:** Dodge Brothers, late '29.

A DAY AT THE RACES

Judy: Doctor, I'm happy to welcome you as chief of staff. I hope you'll be able to pull the sanitarium out of its difficulties.

Mrs. Upjohn: Oh, the Sanitarium is having a little financial trouble.

Hackenbush: I get it. I'm not going to get paid, huh? Well, so long, boys.

Mrs. Upjohn: Oh, no—no—no, Doctor—please don't go. I'll take care of your salary.

A DAY AT THE RACES

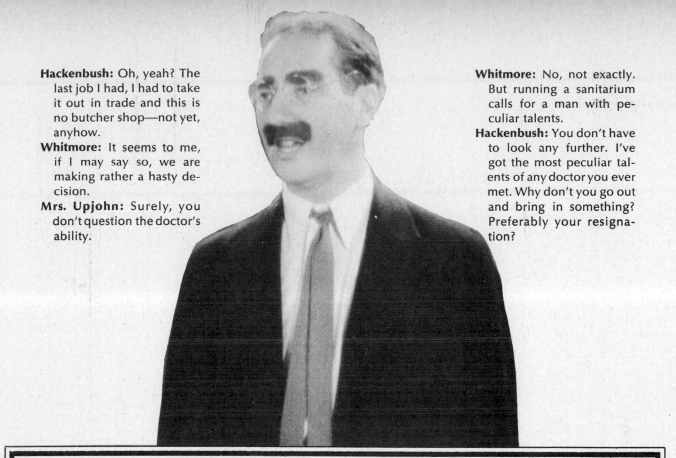

Hackenbush: Oh, yeah? The last job I had, I had to take it out in trade and this is no butcher shop—not yet, anyhow.

Whitmore: It seems to me, if I may say so, we are making rather a hasty decision.

Mrs. Upjohn: Surely, you don't question the doctor's ability.

Whitmore: No, not exactly. But running a sanitarium calls for a man with peculiar talents.

Hackenbush: You don't have to look any further. I've got the most peculiar talents of any doctor you ever met. Why don't you go out and bring in something? Preferably your resignation?

Whitmore: Tell me, Dr. Hackenbush, just what was your medical background?

Hackenbush: Medically?

Whitmore: Yes.

Hackenbush: Well, uh, at the age of fifteen I got a job in a drugstore filling prescriptions.

Whitmore: Don't you have to be twenty-one to fill prescriptions?

Hackenbush: Well, ah, that's for grown ups. I just filled them for children.

Whitmore: No, no, Doctor. I mean where did you get your training as a physician?

Hackenbush: Oh, well to begin with I took four years at Vassar.

Mrs. Upjohn: Vassar? But that's a girls' college.

Hackenbush: I found that out the third year. I'd've been there yet but I went out for the swimming team.

Whitmore: The Doctor seems reluctant to discuss his medical experiences.

Hackenbush: Well, medically, my experiences have been most unexciting except during the flu epidemic.

Whitmore: Ah, and what happened?

Hackenbush: I got the flu.

Mrs. Upjohn: Oh, doctor, I think it's time for my pill.

241

Hackenbush: Ixnay on the opeday.
Mrs. Upjohn: Now you told me to take them regularly.
Whitmore: Just a minute, Mrs. Upjohn, that looks like a horsepill to me.
Hackenbush: Oh, you've taken them before?

Mrs. Upjohn: Are you sure, Doctor, you haven't made a mistake?
Hackenbush: You have nothing to worry about. The last patient I gave one of those to won the Kentucky Derby.
Whitmore: Uh, may I examine this, please?

Whitmore: Do you actually give those to your patients? Isn't that awfully large for a pill?

Hackenbush: No. It was too small for a basketball and I didn't know what to do with it. Say, you're awfully large for a pill yourself.

A DAY AT THE RACES

Whitmore: Dr. Wilmerding, just what is your opinion?

Wilmerding: It must take a lot of water to swallow that.

Hackenbush: Nonsense, you can swallow that with five gallons.

Whitmore: Isn't that a lot of water for a patient to take?

Hackenbush: Not if the patient has a bridge in her mouth. You see the water flows under the bridge and the patient walks over the bridge and meets the pill on the other side.

ANOTHER LOVE SCENE

Tony (Chico), in need of money for a bet, decides to sucker Dr. Hackenbush into supplying the cash.

Tony: Get your ice cream.
Hackenbush: Two dollars on Sun-Up.
Tony: Hey. Hey, boss. Come here. You wanta something hot?
Hackenbush: Not now, I just had lunch. Anyhow, I don't like hot ice cream.

Hackenbush: No. Some other time. I'm sorry, I'm betting on Sun-Up. Some other time, eh? Two dollars on Sun-Up.
Tony: Hey, come here. I no sell ice cream. That's a fake to foola the police. I sella tips on the horses. I gotta something today can't lose. One dollar.

Tony: Hey, come here. Sun-Up is the worse horse on the track.
Hackenbush: I notice he wins all the time.
Tony: Aw, that's just because he comes in first.
Hackenbush: Well, I don't want him any better than first.

Tony: Hey, boss, come here. Come here. Suppose you bet on Sun-Up. What you gonna get for your money? Two to one. One dollar and you remember me all your life.

Hackenbush: That's the most nauseating proposition I've ever had.

Tony: Come on, come on, you look like a sport. Come on, boss—Don't be a crunger for one buck. Thank you.

Hackenbush: What's this?

Tony: That'sa the horse.

Hackenbush: How'd he get in here?

Tony: Get your ice cream. Tootsie-fruitsie ice cream.

A DAY AT THE RACES

Hackenbush: Z . . . V-B-X-R-P-L. I had that same horse when I had my eyes examined. Hey, ice cream.

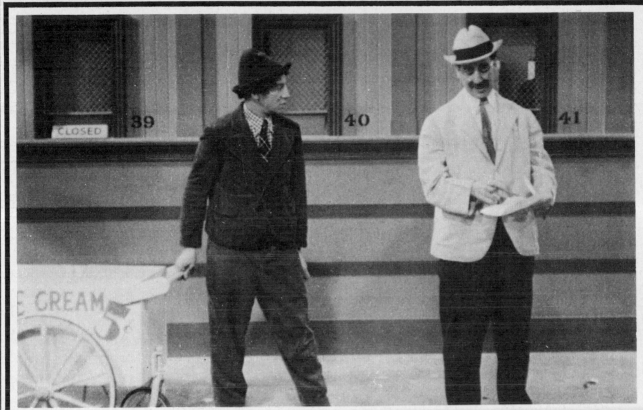

Hackenbush: What about this optical illusion you just slipped me? I don't understand it.

Tony: Oh, that's not the real name of the horse, that's the name of the horse's code. Look in your code book.

Hackenbush: What do you mean, code?

Tony: Yeah, look in the code book. That'll tell you what horse you got.

Hackenbush: Well, I haven't got any code book.

Tony: You no got a code book?

Hackenbush: You know where I can get one?

Tony: Well, just by accident I think I got one here. Here you are.

Hackenbush: How much is it?

Tony: That's free.

Hackenbush: Oh, thanks.

Tony: Just a one dollar printing charge.

Hackenbush: Well, give me one without printing, I'm sick of printing.

Tony: Aw, come on, you want to win.

Hackenbush: Yeah, sure, of course I want to win.

Tony: Well, then you got to have this.

Hackenbush: I want to win but I don't want the savings of a lifetime wiped out in a twinkling of an eye. Here.

Tony: Thank you very much. Ice cream.

Hackenbush: Z-v-b-x-r-p-l. Page 34. Hey, ice cream, I can't make head or tail out of this.

Tony: Oh, that's all right, look in the master code book . . . that'll tell you where to look.
Hackenbush: Master code? I haven't got any master code book.
Tony: You no got a master code book?
Hackenbush: No . . . do you know where I can get one?

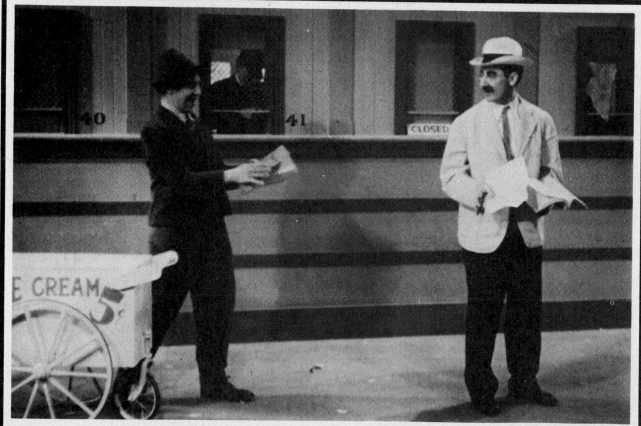

Tony: Well, just by accident I think I got one right here . . . huh—here you are. . . .

Hackenbush: Lot of quick accidents around here for a quiet neighborhood.

A DAY AT THE RACES

Hackenbush: Just a minute, ah is there a printing charge on this?

Tony: No. . . .

Hackenbush: Oh, thanks. . .

Tony: Just a two dollar delivery charge. . . .

Hackenbush: What do you mean delivery charge, I'm standing right next to you.

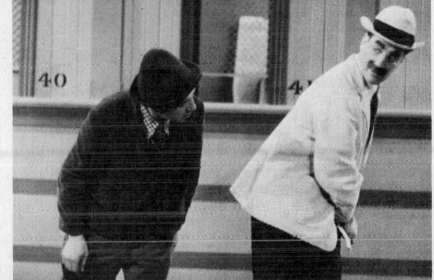

Tony: Well, for such a short distance, I make it a dollar.

Hackenbush: Couldn't I move over here and make it uh—fifty cents?

Tony: Yes, but I'd move over here and make it a dollar just the same.

Hackenbush: Say, maybe I better open a charge account . . . huh?

Tony: You gotta some references?

Hackenbush: Well, the only one I know around here is you.

Tony: That's no good . . . you'll have to pay cash.

Hackenbush: You know a little while ago I could have put two dollars on—Sun-Up and have avoided all this.

Tony: Yeah, I know . . . throw your money away. . . . Thank you very much.

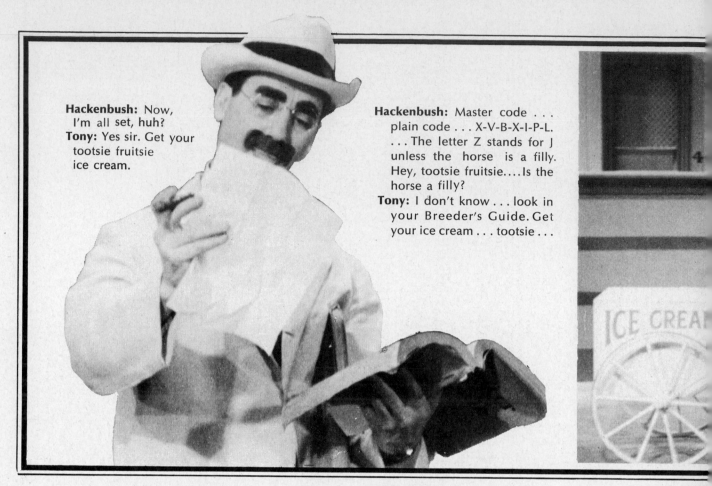

Hackenbush: Now, I'm all set, huh?
Tony: Yes sir. Get your tootsie fruitsie ice cream.

Hackenbush: Master code . . . plain code . . . X-V-B-X-I-P-L. . . . The letter Z stands for J unless the horse is a filly. Hey, tootsie fruitsie. . . . Is the horse a filly?
Tony: I don't know . . . look in your Breeder's Guide. Get your ice cream . . . tootsie . . .

Hackenbush: Where can I get one, as though I didn't know.

Tony: One is no good . . . you got to have the whole set. . . . Get your tootsie fruitsie. . . .

Hackenbush: What do you mean, Breeder's Guide? I haven't got a Breeder's Guide.

Tony: You haven't got a Breeder's Guide?

Hackenbush: Not so loud... I don't want it to get around that I haven't got a Breeder's Guide.... Even my best friends don't know I haven't got a Breeder's Guide.

Tony: Well, boss, I feel pretty sorry for you walking around without a Breeder's Guide... why you're just throwing your money away buying those other books without a Breeder's Guide.

Hackenbush: Hey, you know, all I wanted was a horse, not a public library . . . what d'you mean. . . How much is the set?

Tony: One dollar. . . .

Hackenbush: One dollar?

Tony: Yeah . . . four for five.

Hackenbush: Well all right I'll . . . I'll . . . give me the four of them. There's no use throwing away money, eh.

Tony: Oh, yah, here you are.

Hackenbush: This is all I'm buying too, I didn't want so much . . . I thought you could do this quickly.

Tony: There you are.

A DAY AT THE RACES

Tony: Six dollars on Sun-Up.

Tony: Hurry up—tootsie fruitsie ice cream.
Hackenbush: ZVBXRPL is Burns.
Tony: Yeah, that's right.
Hackenbush: Heh, Burns?
Tony: Yeah, yeah. Someday the code gives you the name of the jockey instead of the horse. Now you find out who jockey Burns is riding and that's the horse you bet on. It's easy. Get your Ice Cream, tootsie fruitsie. . . .
Hackenbush: Oh, I'm . . . I'm gettin' the idea of it. . . .

Hackenbush: . . . I didn't get it for a long time you know. It's pretty tricky when you don't know it, isn't it, huh?
Tony: It's not that book.
Hackenbush: Huh?
Tony: It's not that book.
Hackenbush: It's not — it's not that book . . .

Tony: No.
Hackenbush: Oh, I see.
Tony: No, it's not that book.
Hackenbush: Huh?

Tony: It's not that book . . . . . Nope . . . nope, it's not that book . . . No, you haven't got that book.
Hackenbush: You've got it huh? I'll get it in a minute, though won't I?

255

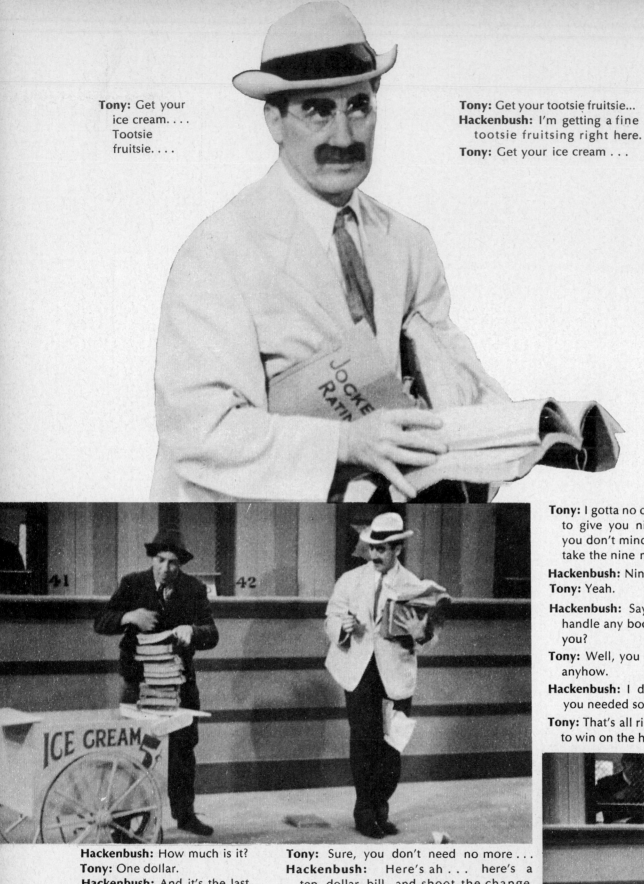

Tony: Get your
ice cream. . . .
Tootsie
fruitsie. . . .

Tony: Get your tootsie fruitsie...
Hackenbush: I'm getting a fine
tootsie fruitsing right here.
Tony: Get your ice cream . . .

Tony: I gotta no change... I'll have
to give you nine more books,
you don't mind, huh, boss? You
take the nine more books.

Hackenbush: Nine more . . .
Tony: Yeah.

Hackenbush: Say, you don't
handle any bookcases there, do
you?

Tony: Well, you come tomorrow,
anyhow.

Hackenbush: I didn't know that
you needed so many.

Tony: That's all right, you're going
to win on the horses today.

Hackenbush: How much is it?
Tony: One dollar.
Hackenbush: And it's the last
book I'm buying.

Tony: Sure, you don't need no more . . .
Hackenbush: Here's ah . . . here's a
ten dollar bill, and shoot the change,
will you they're going to the post .

Tony: I'll find it, here it is, here it is . . . Right here . . .

Hackenbush: I just heard the fellow blowing his horn.

Tony: Here it is, here . . . Jockey Burns—hundred and fifty two... . . . that's Rosie . . .

Hackenbush: Rosie, huh?

Tony: Sure . . . oh, boy, look . . . forty to one . . .

Hackenbush: Forty to one.

Tony: Oh, what a horse, Rosie . . . look . . .

Hackenbush: Am I going to give that bookie a whipping . . .

Tony: Oh, boy . . .

Hackenbush: I was going to bet on Sun-Up...at ten to one...

Hackenbush: . . . just walk up and bet on a horse.

Tony: Yeah. Open . . .

Hackenbush: Huh?

Tony: Open . . . open . . . close . . .

Hackenbush: Say, am I shedding books down there?

Tony: Close.

Hackenbush: Huh?

Tony: Close . . . that's it. Now . . .

Hackenbush: Good thing I brought my legs with me, huh?

Tony: Yeah, yeah.

Hackenbush: Tell me what horse have I got . . . hurry up, will you?

Tony: Look . . . forty to one . . . that's it . . .

A DAY AT THE RACES

257

Hackenbush: I'll show them a thing or two . . . Say there . . . big boy, two dollars on Rosie, huh?
Bookie: Sorry, that race is over . . .

Hackenbush: Huh?
Bookie: I say that race is over . . .
Hackenbush: Over . . . who won?
Bookie: Sun-Up . . .

Tony: Sun-Up! That's ah my horse . . . Sun-Up . . .

Tony: Sun-Up! Sun-Up! Hurry ... good ah by boss ... ten ... twenty ... thirty ...

Hackenbush: Get your tootsie fruitsie nice ice cream ... nice tootsie fruitsie ice cream ...

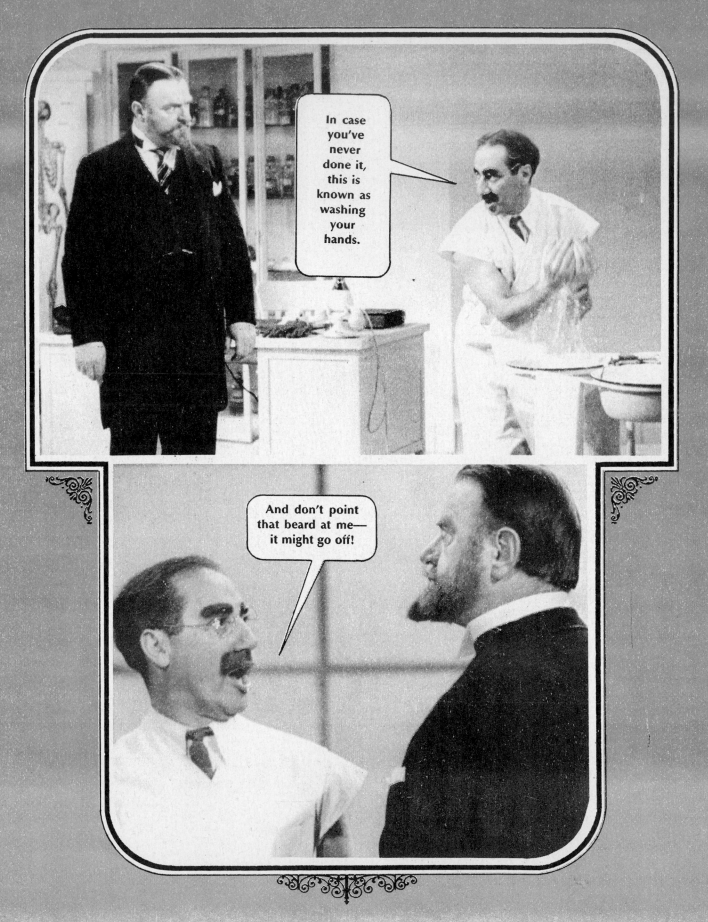

Dr. Hackenbush has a wonderful evening planned. Naturally the evening revolves around a girl, Flo, whom he intends to wine and dine, etc. Tony and Stuffy (Harpo) are aware that Flo is trying to blackmail the good Doctor and attempt to disrupt his plans.

Flo: Oh, Doctor. Thank you.
Hackenbush: Thank you. Do you like gardenias?
Flo: I adore them. How did you know?

Hackenbush: I didn't—so I got you a forget-me-not. One whiff of this and you'll forget everything.

Hackenbush: Won't you sit down?
Flo: Thank yo.
Hackenbush: Thank yo.

Flo: Oh, a—do you mind?
Hackenbush: Not at all. I always take the wrap.
Flo: You're such a charming host.

Hackenbush: The Hackenbushes were all like that. How about a short beer?
Flo: Nothing, thank you.
Hackenbush: Thank yo.

Hackenbush: Ah, Miss Marlowe, I've dreamed of this moment ever since I met you. For days I've been trying to see you. And I still! don't seem to be able to make the grade. Ah, a quiet evening alone with you. What more could anyone ask?
Hackenbush: Say, have you sneaked out of here?

Hackenbush: Oh, there you are.

Flo: Yoo hoo.

Hackenbush: Yoo hoo. Isn't this too, too devastating? Would you mind carving? I can't reach the steak from here.

Flo: Me?

Hackenbush: Yes?
Tony: Hey, Doc! Can you see us?

Hackenbush: If I can't there's something wrong with my glasses.
Tony: You mean her? She's the one? We fix her.

Tony: Ah, signorina, gentile e bella. Oh, baby, you looka good to me.
Flo: Oh, oh—oh, stop it.
Hackenbush: Hey, wait a minute, wait a minute. I thought you came here to see me?
Tony: Well, I can see you from here.
Flo: Oh, oh, get up, you . . . oh, oh. . . .
Tony: You know my friend.

Hackenbush: No, no. Not for me— three men on a horse.

Flo: Oh, what is the meaning of this? Oh, why you little pest. Well!

Hackenbush: Say, what's the matter with you muggs. Haven't you got any gallantry at all?

Tony: She's in with Whitmore. She's trying to frame you.

Hackenbush: I wouldn't mind framing her. A prettier picture I've never seen.

Flo: Thank you.

Hackenbush: Thank yo.

Tony: Hey Doc! Doc, I'm tell you a secret—she's out to get you.

Flo: Why, I've never been so insulted in my life.

Hackenbush: Well, it's early yet.

Flo: Well, I'm leaving. I'm certainly not going to stay here with these men.

Hackenbush: You're not leaving—they're leaving. Now come on, I want you fellows to get out of here.

Flo: Oh, my cape.

Hackenbush: Come back here with my woman.

Flo: Oh! . . . .

Hackenbush: You fellows are busting up a beautiful romance. What's the matter with you.

Tony: Doc, get her out—she's gonna make trouble.

Hackenbush: You've got her all wrong. This is my aunt and she's come to talk over some old family matters.

Tony: I wish I had an aunt look like that.

Hackenbush: Well, take it up with your uncle.

Tony: Doc. You're playing with fire.

Hackenbush: I notice you didn't mind getting scorched.

Tony: Well, I got fire insurance.

Hackenbush: Well, you better get accident.

Flo: Scram! Blow! Oh!

Flo: Oh! Oh! Oh!

A DAY AT THE RACES

267

Hackenbush: How do you
like those cheap chiselers
horning in on us.
Flo: Thank you.
Hackenbush: Thank yo.

Flo: Oh a — how about a
little scotch?
Hackenbush: Why, I'd love it.
Oh, a—I'll ring for some.
Flo: Thank yo.
Hackenbush: Thank yo.

Hackenbush: Will you have the
bell-hop hop up with some hop
scotch?

Hackenbush: I'll flip you to see who pays for it.   **Flo:** Oh, Doctor.

Tony: I'm O'Reilly, the house detective.

Hackenbush: Don't talk so loud—your mustache will drop off.

Tony: Have you got a woman here?

Hackenbush: If I haven't, I've wasted thirty minutes of valuable time!

Tony: Well, you better get her out of here! This is the last time I'm going to tell you.

Hackenbush: The last time? Can I depend on that?

Tony: Yes, because this time I'm going to stay all night. This looks like a tough case.

Hackenbush: So does this!

Tony: I think I'll call my assistant.

A DAY AT THE RACES

Flo: Oh!
Hackenbush: If you're looking for my fingerprints, you're a little early!

A DAY AT THE RACES

ANOTHER LOVE SCENE

Flo:
I want to be near you.
I want you to hold me.
Oh! Hold me closer! Closer! Closer!

Hackenbush: If I hold you
any closer I'll be in
back of you!

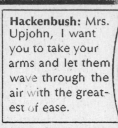

Hackenbush: Mrs. Upjohn, I want you to take your arms and let them wave through the air with the greatest of ease.

Mrs. Upjohn: How long do you want me to do this, Doctor.
Hackenbush: Just until you fly away.

Pick me up at 5!

AT THE CIRCUS

Driver: Hey, mister. Eighteen seventy-five.
Loophole: Eighteen seventy-five! That's what I thought. The 1940 models run much smoother.

Loophole: You know, if you hadn't sent for me, I'd probably be home now in a nice warm bedroom, in a comfortable bed with a hot toddy.

Antonio: Huh?

Loophole: That's a drink!

Antonio: That's-a-too bad.

Loophole: I'll bet your father spent the first year of your life throwing rocks at the stork.

ANOTHER LOVE SCENE

**J. Cheever Loophole (Groucho)
crashes the home of an old flame (Margaret Dumont).
If only she remembered him.**

Mrs. D.: Well, I . . .

Loophole: I know, you have forgotten those June nights on the Riviera, where we sat 'neath the shimmering skies! Moonlight bathing in the Mediterranean! We were young, gay, reckless! The night I drank champagne from your slipper—two quarts. It would have held more, but you were wearing inner soles! Oh, Hildegarde!

Mrs. D.: My name is Suzanna!

Loophole: Let's not quibble! It's enough that you've killed something fine and beautiful! Oh Suzanna . . . Oh, Suzanna. Oh, won't you fly with me, for I need ten thousand dollars, 'cause the sheriff's after me!

Mrs. D.: Get out of this room or I'll scream for the servants!

Loophole: Let the servants know! Let the whole world know about us!

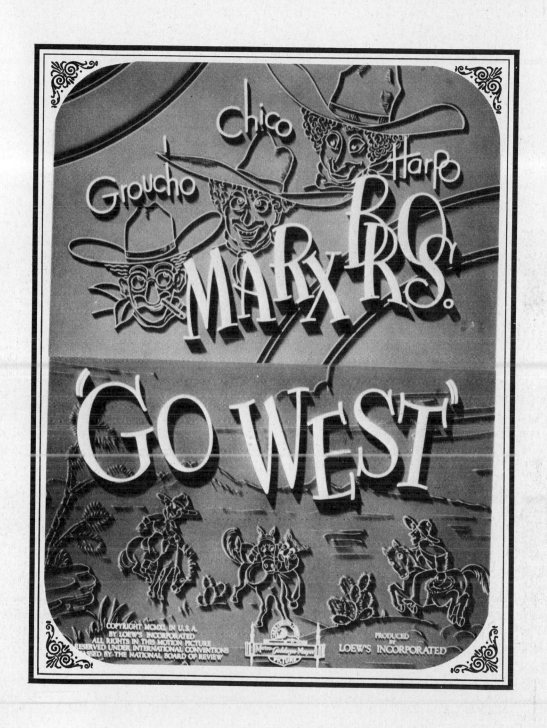

Quale: Say, where'd I see your face before?

Joe: Right where it is now.

Quale: Madame, why is that baby constantly crying?

Woman: He can't stand the jerks in the coach.

S. Quentin Quale (Groucho), short of cash, tries to hustle a few bucks from Rusty (Harpo) and Joseph Panello (Chico).

Joe (Chico): Hey, Mister. Is this the right way for my brother to get on the train for the West?

Quale (Groucho): Not unless they're throwing a masquerade party out West, it isn't.

Joe: All we want to know is where is the train?

Quale: The train? It's out on the tracks. It seldom comes in here.

Joe: Come on, Rusty. I buy you a ticket. Where's your seventy dollars? You only got ten? What you do with the other sixty? Oh, you buy a snake, huh? Well, I don't know how I'm gonna get you a ticket. You ain't got enough money.

Quale: Money? So you two gents are heading West, eh, pardner?

Joe: Not me—just my brother. You see, I gotta no money. So he's goin' West, and when he gets off the train he's gonna pick up some gold and send it to me. They say that the gold is layin' all over the streets. Eh, Rusty? All over the streets you find the gold.

Quale: The way he's dressed, he looks like he was layin' all over the streets. Of course, the gold is layin' all over the streets, but they won't let him take any. Ha! He's a tenderfoot!

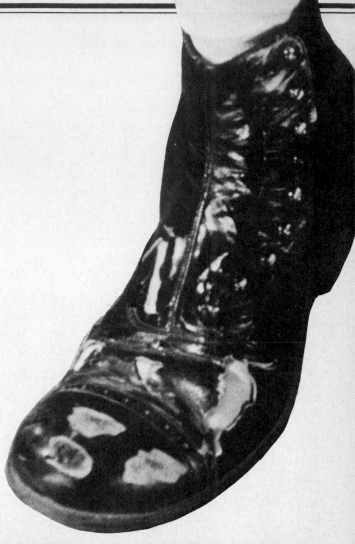

Joe: You wear those shoes you gotta tender foot, too.

Quale: Oh, those are...shoes? I thought that was fungus with buttons.

Joe: All right . . . all right! Suppose he's gotta tender feet! You don't pick up the gold with the feet!

Quale: No, you don't understand, my friend. A tenderfoot is an Easterner, and out West they shoot at anything that looks Eastern. Why, they'll blow his head off if he goes out West with that flea incubator.

Joe: What's the matter with that hat? That hat cost a lot of money.

Quale: How much did it cost him?

Joe: I don't know. He stole it.

Quale: Now, wait a minute, wait a minute. I'm just trying to save his life. You love your brother, don't you?

Joe: No, but I'm used to him.

Quale: Now, this is the kind of hat they're wearing this season. This is the 1870 model. It's what they call the pioneer's cap.

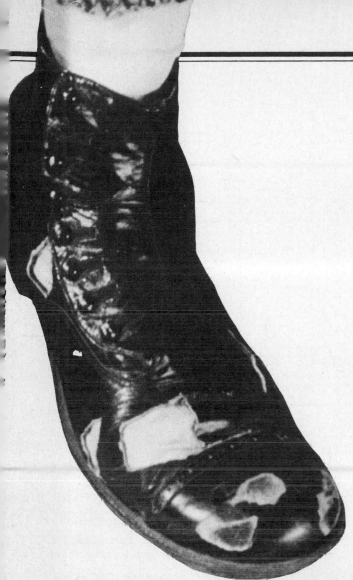

Joe: Isn't that tail supposed to be in the back?

Quale: Not on him. That's genuine beaver.

Joe: Pretty.

Quale: No, I—I'll stroke it. It's still my hat, you know. That'll be ten dollars.

Joe: Ten dollars you want for that old beaver?

Quale: I'm not in business for love, you know. I was in love once, and I got the business. But that's another story, and a very unpleasant one, too.

Joe: Why should he buy a hat? He ain't even got enough money for a ticket.

Quale: Look, you can always get a ticket, but this is the last hat of its kind. The beavers have stopped makin' 'em. They're all out playing football. Ten dollars.

Joe: Well, he's a poor boy. He'll give you a dollar. Will you take it?

Quale: Well, I'll take it, but I'm only makin' a buck on it.

Quale: Why don't you let me go? Let's keep this a perfect memory, and someday this bitter ache shall pass, my sweet. Time wounds all heals. You know, there's a drunk sitting at the first table who looks exactly like you—and one who looks exactly like me. Dull, isn't it? He's so full of alcohol, if you put a lighted wick in his mouth, he'd burn for three days.

Quale: How would you like a little necklace that formerly belonged to the Czarina of Russia?

Indian Woman: No like—me want Cadillac sedan.
Quale: She's been off the reservation!

How the west was won.

Quale: Panello, this Indian is no Indian!

Joe: If he's no Indian, why is he wearin' a chicken for a hat?

Quale: Oh, stop it! Trying to pass yourself off as a red man. Why, you can't even speak the language. Let me hear you recite Hiawatha by Henry Wadsworth Longfellow.

Indian Chief: Ugh.

Joe: That's not it.

Quale: If it is, they've shortened it since I went to school. And you call yourself a red man.

Indian: White man talk too much. Make Chief heap mad.

Quale: White man red man's friend. White man want to make friends with red brother.

Joe: And sister, too.

Quale: Are you insinuating that the white man is not the Indian's friend? Ha! Who swindled you out of Manhattan Island for $24?

Joe: White man.

Quale: Who turned you into wood and stood you in front of a cigar store?

Joe: White man.

Quale: Who put your head on a nickel, and then took the nickel away?

Joe: Slot machine.

Quale: Members of the tribe—I rest my case.

Wolf J. Flywheel (Groucho) dusts off his magnifying glass and enters the world of corporate intrigue.

Wolf: Naturally she hired me, the greatest detective since Sherlock Holmes.

Martha: I'm crazy about Sherlock Holmes.

Wolf: It won't do you any good. He's got a wife and three kids.

Grover: So this man is a detective.

Martha: Yes.

Grover: Huh!

Martha: Mr. Flywheel.

Wolf: Just call me, Wolf.

Martha: Now that you've revealed yourself — you've spoiled everything. And after you promised not to tell.

Wolf: How could I keep from telling the world of you and your beauty . . . and my feelings about you?

Wolf: She walks in beauty, like the night of cloudless climes and starry skies.

Martha: Why, that's Byron.

Wolf: He was thinking of you when he wrote it.

Martha: Wolf, do you remember this? Thou friend, whose presence on my wintry heart Fell, like bright Spring upon some herbless plain.

Wolf: Shelley?

Martha: Shelley.

Wolf: They're not writing that kind of stuff anymore. Here's a little something to you. Your eyes so blue. . . . Your heart so true. Your lips divine. Say you'll be mine.

Martha: Oh, where did you ever learn to write such beautiful poetry?

Wolf: I worked five years for Burma Shave.

Grover: What is this man, a detective, a floorwalker or a poet?

Wolf: All three, and not bad at making love—eh, Martha?

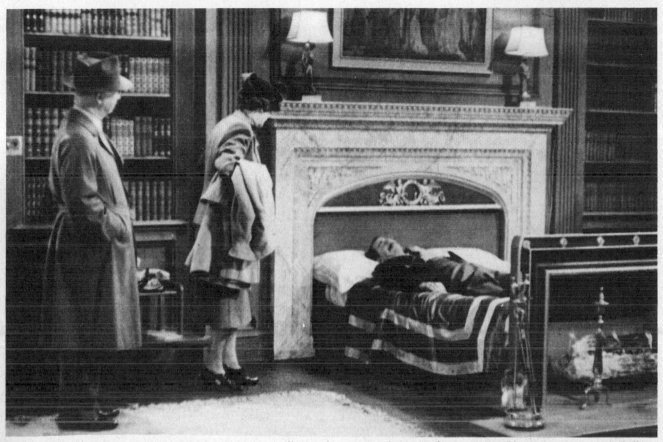

Woman: Pardon me. Mister! Mister! Can you tell me the price of this bed? **Wolf:** Eight thousand dollars.

Woman: Why, that's preposterous! I can get this same bed anywhere in town for twenty-five dollars.
Wolf: Yes, but not with me in it.

Man: Sir! How dare you talk that way to my wife?
Wolf: How dare I talk that way to your wife? Have you ever met me before?
Woman: No!
Wolf: Then why do you allow your wife to go around waking up strange men?
Woman: Oh, come Henry, before you lose your temper.

Wolf: I'll bet he does the cooking.

287

ANOTHER LOVE SCENE

Wolf: Oh, hop in here. There's a few things I'd like to discuss with you. What I am about to say is intended for your ears alone.

Martha: Oh, Wolf!

Wolf: Martha, dear, there are many bonds that will hold us together through eternity.

Martha: Really, Wolf? What are they?

Wolf: Your Government Bonds, your Savings bonds, your Liberty bonds —and maybe in a year or two after we're married—

Martha: Yes?

Wolf: Who knows? There may be a little baby bond.

Martha: Oh, it all seems so wonderful! Tell me, Wolfie, dear, will we have a beautiful home?

Wolf: Of course. You're not planning on moving, are you?

Martha: No. But I'm afraid after we're married a while, a beautiful young girl will come along and—you'll forget all about me.

Wolf: Don't be silly. I'll write you twice a week.

THE BIG STORE